THE
HUMAN
MARGIN

THE
HUMAN
MARGIN

Building the
Foundations of Trust

Katherine Meese, PhD | Quint Studer, MSE

ACHE Management Series

Your board, staff, or clients may also benefit from this book's insight. For information on quantity discounts, contact the Health Administration Press Marketing Manager at (312) 424-9450.

This publication is intended to provide accurate and authoritative information in regard to the subject matter covered. It is sold, or otherwise provided, with the understanding that the publisher is not engaged in rendering professional services. If professional advice or other expert assistance is required, the services of a competent professional should be sought.

The statements and opinions contained in this book are strictly those of the author and do not represent the official positions of the American College of Healthcare Executives or the Foundation of the American College of Healthcare Executives.

28   27   26   25   24   5   4   3   2   1

Library of Congress Cataloging-in-Publication Data

Names: Meese, Katherine A., author. | Studer, Quint, author. | American
    College of Healthcare Executives, issuing body.
Title: The human margin : building the foundations of trust / Katherine A.
    Meese and Quint Studer.
Other titles: Management series (Ann Arbor, Mich.)
Description: Chicago, IL : Health Administration Press, [2024] | Series:
    HAP/ACHE management series | Includes bibliographical references and
    index. | Summary: "Respected researcher Katherine Meese has teamed up
    with Quint Studer, a well-known author and practitioner with more than
    40 years of experience in helping healthcare organizations improve
    performance and become better workplaces. The result is a science-backed
    leadership book that integrates the latest workplace research with
    tactics to create high-performance environments where people can
    flourish. The Human Margin: Building the Foundations of Trust interprets
    new research on what today's healthcare workforce really wants and finds
    that trust in leadership is at the heart of everything"-- Provided by
    publisher.
Identifiers: LCCN 2023046326 | ISBN 9781640554467 (trade paperback ; alk.
    paper) | ISBN 9781640554474 (ebook) | ISBN 9781640554481 (epub)
Subjects: MESH: Health Workforce | Organizational Culture |
    Trust--psychology | Work Engagement | Health Services Administration |
    Leadership
Classification: LCC RA440.9 | NLM W 76.1 | DDC 362.1--dc23/eng/20231207
LC record available at https://lccn.loc.gov/2023046326

The paper used in this publication meets the minimum requirements of American National Standard for Information Sciences—Permanence of Paper for Printed Library Materials, ANSI Z39.48-1984. ∞ ™

Manuscript editor: Kevin McLenithan; Cover designer: Carla Nessa; Layout: PerfecType

Found an error or a typo? We want to know! Please e-mail it to hapbooks@ache.org, mentioning the book's title and putting "Book Error" in the subject line.

For photocopying and copyright information, please contact Copyright Clearance Center at www.copyright.com or at (978) 750-8400.

Health Administration Press
A division of the Foundation of the
    American College of Healthcare Executives
300 S. Riverside Plaza, Suite 1900
Chicago, IL 60606-6698
(312) 424-2800

To my late mother, Janis Lee Carelock—
the nurse who started it all.
Katherine

In 1982 I entered the world of recovery. I became teachable. Thank you to my teachers, the Friends of Bill W., and my mentor, Mark Clement. In 1983 Rishy Long, now Rishy Studer, somehow gave this guy a chance. Since that time, she has been the rock: always kind, always loving, always willing to take a risk in making life better for others, and always willing to love me enough to let me know when I have spinach in my teeth. Love to you, Rishy.
Quint

Contents

Preface

IT's EXCITING TO coauthor this book with Dr. Katherine Meese. Her research on engagement in healthcare and creating cultures where people can flourish is so important, now more than ever. To me, the fact that Katherine broke down the research across different departments in the organization greatly clarifies the specific conditions to maximize the most important capital we have in healthcare: people. Her research shows how the workplace is evolving and challenges some commonly held beliefs around what employees want. For example, money is not as much a factor in retaining employees as has been thought. Because of the impact of the pandemic, trustworthiness of senior leadership is more central to retention than has ever been previously known.

This last point is great news. Healthcare executives have always cared for their teams. The pandemic and other factors in the external environment have made things tough, but through thick and thin, I've watched senior leaders in our industry demonstrate a commitment to the "people" part of healthcare all along.

But what appeals to me the most about this book is how applicable the findings are to midlevel leaders. As we'll discuss later, the individuals in the middle have a tremendous effect on organizational performance. They have always had a tough job (and it's gotten even tougher in recent years) and a passion to do that job well. It is a privilege to be a part of a book that helps organizations invest in these critical players.

Healthcare is a wonderful place to build a lifelong career. My experience is that many people in a supervisory role got there much as I did: The boss quits, and the organization does an internal promotion. A person goes from an hourly or salaried position, where they are an individual contributor, to a supervisory role. This is a good thing, for the people we lead know we are familiar with the job. They also like the fact that, most often, these early-career promotions are internal. My observation is that a great many people in leadership roles learn mostly on the job and through leadership skill development offered via their place of work. As healthcare has become more complex and demanding, it is crucial that organizations fill this important role. Every leader in healthcare in every role is a chief development officer for those they lead.

That said, I applaud the individuals who are fortunate to achieve degrees in healthcare administration early on. These people know how important it is to continue learning. Master of health administration programs add a critical dimension to the knowledge of healthcare professionals.

I am grateful for the opportunity to partner with Katherine in writing *The Human Margin*. I am grateful for all my years of getting to know and learning from practitioners, leaders, and employees at all levels and in all types of organizations. And I am grateful for you, the readers, whose desire to make healthcare better continues to inspire me.

Thank you.

Quint Studer

WHEN I WAS a mother of two young toddlers, I felt that I had read every parenting book on the planet. I was committed to making sure they had sleep, optimally developed brains, and were well-prepared to start a nonprofit by age four for their future college applications.

But where I struggled most was in finding ways to implement the suggestions and philosophies in these parenting books. What do I *actually* say and do in the moment? Explaining brain development and germ theory wasn't working well on my two-year-old. An older mother helped me see the magic of the short catchphrase. Is my kid licking the handrail in the bird section of the zoo?

"Not food."

It was simple, effective, and useful in the moment.

As a new leader, I often found myself in desperate need of a good catchphrase. I knew the big picture of what I was supposed to be doing (kind of) but I needed the right words and tools! As a researcher, my passion is to help distill decades of research, explain it in a relatable way, and offer words, phrases, and tools you can use right now. My approach to this timely and important subject is to ask novel questions and study the findings that arise from them. In our ongoing research, my colleagues and I are constantly collecting data, analyzing it, and exploring the human element of healthcare work. While our goal is always to disseminate our findings through the peer-reviewed literature, that process is lengthy. Part of my goal in creating this book is to get some of these findings into the hands of leaders who are dealing with these issues right now. Interested readers can find more information about our methods in the Appendix at the back of this book.

I am excited to be partnering with Quint Studer on this. Quint has an amazing ability to take complicated ideas and to make them achievable and memorable. Furthermore, his decades of experience in helping organizations improve gives him a remarkable ability to know what types of activities and phrases are likely to work in practice.

I am continually awed and inspired by the dedication, passion, and courage that our healthcare workers display—often despite impossible situations. They are remarkable people. They deserve the best leadership and work environments we can provide so that they can bring their very best to patients and each other. My goal with this book is to help us move a step in that direction.

To our healthcare workers: Thank you for inspiring me daily with your courage and compassion.

All my gratitude,

Katherine Meese

CHAPTER 1

Introduction: The Human Margin

HEALTHCARE IS A very special industry. Unlike professionals in so many other industries, those working in healthcare have a chance to directly affect the lives of others in remarkable ways. One of the many ways healthcare is different from other industries is that the core business is produced not by expensive equipment like offshore oil rigs or factories but by people. Yes, we have fancy equipment, but it is not the tools that produce patient care; it is the people.

In its simplest form, healthcare is humans working with humans to heal humans.[1] Sister Irene Krauss, a nun with the Daughters of Charity, famously coined the phrase "No margin, no mission," which has now become pervasive in the industry. Three margins are typically emphasized when measuring organizational performance:

1. **The financial margin.** Do we have enough money to keep the doors open, pursue our mission, and grow for the future?
2. **The operational margin.** Do we have enough beds, space, speed, supplies, and quality?
3. **The human margin.** Do we have the staff available to meet the needs of the patients and their families?

This book is designed to provide a helpful guide to diagnosing our teammates' needs and creating a path to take the "people piece" to the next level and beyond. As people reevaluate their lives and work, creating healthy environments where employees can thrive is more important than ever.

We define the human margin as having a thriving workforce that is supported in bringing their best selves to one another and to our patients. When we consider the strength of our human margin, here are some questions to ask:

- Are there enough employees to create a sustainable pace of work?
- Can our employees bring their best selves to work?
- Do our employees have enough mental and emotional capacity to bear the inherent stresses of the work and to show empathy in the face of great suffering?
- How do we create an environment for our people to thrive so they can care for our patients and one another?

WHAT WE AIM FOR MATTERS

Organizations know that the goal is more than reducing turnover or burnout. While these are worthy pursuits, we all know we must aim higher.

The mission, vision, and values of an organization convey just that: a mission. Most healthcare mission statements involve some variation on the theme of "we provide the best possible care to people in the community, region, state, or world." To accomplish that, we must have a healthy, vibrant workforce. And for decades now, research has shown a correlation between how employees feel and the care they provide.[2]

We also know that healthcare organizations, and thus their employees, are vital members of the community. Providing healthy work for healthcare employees has always been central to the mission of caring for the health of the community. The healthcare sector is the largest industry nationally.[3] In many areas, healthcare organizations are collectively among the largest employers in the community—it takes many hands to do the work. Our healthcare workforce *is* the community, and the community cannot be healthy without healthy work.

So What Do We Aim For?

We want people to flourish at work so that they can bring their best not only to patients but also to one another. The brain on chronic stress is not optimized for decision-making, which is scary when we think about the complexity of delivering high-quality care. Creating conditions that allow people to flourish at work solves a lot of problems. We increase our chances of delivering the best care, set our caregivers up to create a great experience for one another, and keep our human margin healthy now and for years to come. Healthcare workers tell their friends and children to join the special industry of healthcare, and our future looks a little brighter.

If we want our people to flourish, there are a few ways to get there. Seligman's PERMA model of flourishing suggests that people need the following basic elements to flourish:

- P—Positive emotions such as happiness, gratitude, and hope
- E—Engagement (being fully immersed in our work or being in a state of flow)
- R—Relationships that are healthy and nurturing
- M—Meaning and purpose
- A—Achievement[4]

The great news is that, relative to other industries, healthcare gets an A+ on meaning and purpose. The opportunities to directly affect another person's life and change it for the better arise multiple times a day, often with immediate evidence of the impact. It is incredible. Our research shows that 89 percent of caregivers (including nonclinical employees and leaders) find their work meaningful.[5] For most, it is a *calling*.[6]

Because people are so purpose driven, they keep going even when it would be good to seek help. Clinical training is rigorous and long. When times get hard, we tend to stick it out because we want to stay connected to our calling. Caregivers are so committed to the cause that they will often sacrifice their own well-being and boundaries to serve patients. This is not sustainable, and meaning and purpose ultimately aren't enough to counteract broken systems. You might think of this as a "purpose penalty." Our own data show that although a sense of meaning and purpose will help people stay in their jobs, the effect is not strong enough to counter burnout, negative cultures, and poor working conditions. Burnout was the number-one reason people intended to leave; a lack of meaning in work was ranked ninth.[7]

Because of the COVID-19 pandemic, intense documentation required of healthcare providers, and payer shortfalls, increasing numbers of physicians, nurses, and other caregivers are planning to leave their organizations and, in many cases, the healthcare field altogether. The exodus of one physician from the industry takes a minimum of 12 years to replace, and a bachelor's-prepared nurse takes four. An entire generation of high-school and early-college students is preparing to enter the workforce. What careers will they choose? Ensuring that our human margin remains intact is one of the grandest challenges of healthcare.

Our 2020 survey of healthcare workers asked what would improve their well-being or experience at work. One response stood out:

"To feel that I am not expendable."

We all know how important healthcare workers are. Even when we've done our best to care for our people, we need an even greater focus on the human margin than ever before because of all the aforementioned external factors. Our future depends on it.

Every person in healthcare plays a role in shaping the experiences of their colleagues, but the role of leaders is especially important.

Midlevel leaders are the key to great performance. By "midlevel leaders" we mean all the leaders between the senior executive team and the frontline employees, both clinical and nonclinical. They hold titles such as director, manager, and supervisor.

In general, leaders usually considered to be in the middle are not in the C-suite. However, even people in the C-suite can find themselves situated between the CEO and others. CEOs can feel that they are in the middle between their leadership team and the Board. The key is for all people in a leadership role to attain the skills needed for their specific role. The organization with the best midlevel leadership team wins. Why?

- They affect a higher number of people than any other group. The vast majority of workers in an organization report to someone in the middle.
- They have a huge impact on attracting and retaining talent and shaping how people feel about their jobs.
- They are the eyes and ears on the ground. They know where the performance problems are, and they know who is doing well. They know which processes need fixing.
- They are responsible for bringing out the best in people. They inspire and nurture creativity, innovation, and teamwork. They look for potential mental health issues, broach sensitive conversations, and steer people to the right resources.
- They lead people through crises and keep them focused on mission and purpose.
- They make change happen. Because they're the ones who roll out initiatives from senior leaders, they need to understand the psychology of change and move people through the various stages.
- Finally, they have a tremendous influence on how everyone else views the entire organization.

BEING IN THE MIDDLE IS HARDER THAN EVER

Though midlevel leaders are well positioned to make a huge difference, they have an incredibly tough job and—more often than not—very little training. Leadership is complex for everyone but especially for those in the middle. There is more pressure for results, more need to support struggling employees, more turnover, more retention issues. Midlevel leaders are perpetually asked to do more with less. They are expected to navigate a maze of demands and meet the needs of diverse stakeholders.

The pressure comes from all directions. Leaders in the middle are asked to produce results and make sure senior leadership is happy while also meeting the needs of employees and patients. They have the tough balancing act of building rapport with their team while also needing some distance to maintain professionalism. They may lack clear expectations, resources, or the skills and knowledge to hit the metrics they're being asked to hit.

Yet even with all these leaders' responsibilities and pressures, organizations don't always invest in this group in the way they need and deserve. Many great educational programs exist to prepare someone for a leadership role in healthcare, yet only a small percentage of those in a leadership position have a degree in healthcare management.

What about the rest? We are reminded of a joke: *What is the difference between a person in a staff role on Friday and a leader on Monday? A weekend to think about it.* People often feel thrown into a leadership role with little preparation. If a person balks, their leader might say, "Can you help us out in the interim?" Healthcare people are team players, so they usually say yes to the interim role, but they may not have the opportunity to get the skills and training they need to perform well.

Healthcare is turbulent and fast-paced, and the environment is changing constantly and rapidly. New leaders or leaders in a new role quickly find themselves in unfamiliar territory. Each role brings additional opportunities and requires the leader to take their skills to the next level.

WE'VE REACHED A TIPPING POINT

Midlevel leaders are beginning to buckle under the pressures they face. The pressure is taking a toll on their mental health. We found that in every clinical and nonclinical category, people with supervisory responsibilities were more stressed compared to those who did not manage others. Furthermore, the research laid out in this book makes it clear that a significant gap exists between what C-suite leaders are doing and what the front line *thinks* they are doing. Only the leaders in the middle can close that trust gap.

Research shows that *trust in senior leadership* and *organizational support* are very important for retaining employees.[7] The perception of trust and support involves a combination of senior-leader behaviors and communication in addition to how leaders in the middle shape employee perceptions of what is happening at the top of the organization. Senior leaders can help those in the middle to share vital information with their direct reports and to respond to their questions. In addition, training leaders is one of the most important investments a CEO can make in their teams. If midlevel leaders do not feel supported and equipped, they might unintentionally portray the senior team (and thus the organization) in a less-than-positive way.

To understand why the organization with the strongest midlevel leader team will always perform the best, look at the numbers in your organization. Start with the number of employees who are not in a leadership role. Do the same with the number of employees who have a leadership role but are not in the C-suite. Then calculate the number of people in senior leadership. You will find that a large percentage of the workforce reports directly to someone who is not in senior leadership. The biggest influence on workers' feelings about the organization is the person to whom they report.

The biggest impact on the strength of those in the middle comes from the organization's commitment to their skill and career development. That is whom this book is focused on: those vital difference makers in the middle. It is our hope that the tips and tactics we share will help these already-talented individuals get even better at creating the conditions that enable healthcare's best and brightest to flourish and thrive.

If you are in the C-suite and are reading this, you know how important skill development was for you. This is particularly true for those who are not in a position to receive formal education such as a bachelor's or master's degree in healthcare administration, public health, or business administration. This book will assist you in paying it forward to your midlevel leaders.

For those who are not yet in management, this book is meant to make the transition easier. Not easy, for leadership is never easy (particularly at first), but easier.

For those in the middle, this book is an indication of the love and respect we have for you. Never underestimate the difference you make.

THE APPROACH

Our goal is to support leaders in using an evidence-based approach to maximizing the human margin. We aim to briefly explain the relevant research; apply it to real life; and provide words, phrases, and tools you can use right now.

Behaviors can be predicted. When we understand how our brains, motivations, and reactions work, we can navigate logically and get the results we want for ourselves and our teams. However, even though we have spent most of our lives interacting in human relationships, navigating them is not always intuitive. The great news is that there are equations to help us understand.

The book will combine findings from the academic literature in many industries, as well as original research, with over 10,000 observations that chronicle the healthcare employee experience over the course of several years. You can read more about the research design and approach in the peer-reviewed articles about the research (see Appendix). Two themes arising from this research highlight the importance of this approach.

First, what people *say* is the cause of their intent to leave the organization (wages and compensation) may be different from what factors statistically predict their such intentions (trust). Without an understanding of the science, it is easy to act on what people are saying rather than on what is most likely to fix the problem. Second, the data show that leaders themselves are at high risk for burnout and distress, so they need support in addressing the growing challenges we face in the workplace. Financial resources are thin and stakes are high, so leaders cannot afford to operate in the absence of evidence.

If you work in healthcare, we believe that you genuinely want to help others and do the right thing. Figuring out what to do and how to do it is often more challenging. When we ask people to focus on fewer things, those things can be consistently executed, they will happen more frequently, and the results will be better.

Less = consistency = always = better outcomes

Healthcare is a team sport. Throughout the book, we will use the term "caregivers" or "employees" to refer to anyone in the healthcare organization's workforce, both clinical and nonclinical. We will use the term "clinicians" to refer to those who are specifically involved in direct patient care.

After working with and studying caregivers for many years, we remain awed by their passion and commitment to serving their patients despite impossible conditions and personal sacrifices. We want to help those passionate and dedicated people reduce friction in their work and strengthen their connection to the purpose and meaning in healthcare by having the right tools at their disposal.

We will start with a brief survey of external forces that complicate the human margin and a high-level overview of the research related to well-being, recruitment, and retention of the healthcare workforce.

There are so many findings from the research that we would love to write about. However, we decided to zero in on the things we feel have the best chance of having an effect today. For now, we've created a book that's helpful and informative without being overwhelming. The remainder of the book will focus on specific elements that have the best chance of improving our human margin, based on our own original research and on decades of scholarship on human behavior and motivation:

- Trust
- Communication
- Belonging
- Recognition
- Fairness
- Autonomy
- Well-being
- Peers/coworkers/healthy teams
- Leadership development
- Change management

We will explain each concept, give an overview of what we know from the research literature, and close with what you can do and say right now to improve that element in your teams. Let's jump in!

REFERENCES

1. Meese, K. A., and D. A. Rogers. 2023. "Humans Working with Humans to Heal Humans." In *Leadership in Healthcare: Essential Values and Skills*, 4th ed., C. Dye (ed.). Chicago: Health Administration Press.

2. Salyers, M. P., K. A. Bonfils, L. Luther, R. L. Firmin, D. A. White, E. L. Adams, and A. L. Rollins. 2017. "The Relationship Between Professional Burnout and Quality and Safety in Healthcare: A Meta-analysis." *Journal of General Internal Medicine* 32(4): 475–82.

3. Dowell, E. K. P. 2020. "Census Bureau's 2018 County Business Patterns Provides Data on over 1,200 Industries." United States Census Bureau. Published October 14. http://census.gov/library/stories/2020/10/health-care-still-largest-united-states-employer.html.

4. Seligman, M. 2018. "PERMA and the Building Blocks of Well-Being." *Journal of Positive Psychology* 13(4): 333–35.

5. Meese, K. A., A. Colón-López, J. A. Singh, G. A. Burkholder, and D. A. Rogers. 2021. "Healthcare Is a Team Sport: Stress, Resilience, and Correlates of Well-Being Among Health System Employees in a Crisis." *Journal of Healthcare Management* 66(4): 304–22.

6. Studer, Q. 2021. *The Calling: Why Healthcare Is So Special.* Pensacola, FL: Gratitude Group Publishing.

7. Meese, K. A., L. Boitet, A. Gorman, N. Patel, L. Nassetta, and D. A. Rogers. 2023. "Don't Go: Examining the Relationships Between Purpose, Work Environment and Turnover Intention Across the Entire Healthcare Team." Dublin: European Academy of Management annual meeting.

CHAPTER 2

Things Are Changing

WE WILL REVIEW the state of the healthcare workforce and some of the external trends that will continue into the future. Most of this book focuses on what happens within the walls of the organization, but we need to spend a little time explaining broader environmental trends that are putting organizations in a pressure cooker when it comes to the human margin.

If a nurse leaves my organization for another, that is *my* problem. If a nurse leaves the healthcare workforce altogether, that is *our* problem. Understanding these external forces helps us grasp what features contribute to the intense competition for human capital.

MORTALITY SALIENCE

Mortality salience is the feeling that death is inevitable.[1,2] This is a fact of life, but sometimes death feels closer or further away. When death is brought to our attention, it causes us to reevaluate how we are living. For example, when somebody you know dies, you may think, "Wow. Life is short. How am I going to spend it?"

The Latin term is *memento mori*, which literally means, "Remember that you [have to] die." It is a practice of Stoic philosophers and many religions that reflecting on the possibility of our eventual death changes that way we approach life, often spurring us to "seize the day."

Healthcare workers are reminded of this often in the normal course of their work when they are exposed to tragedy, death, and suffering. However, the COVID-19 pandemic amplified this in a major way for all of society—not only healthcare workers.

Most people had at least an acquaintance or family member who became severely ill or died from COVID—mortality salience went up. It was worse for healthcare workers. Hospitals were overflowing with critically ill patients, and both patients and employees were dying— often much younger than expected. Odds were that if you worked in healthcare during this time, you were reminded of death—a lot.

This left us as a society collectively evaluating our lives and work. When thinking about how to make the most of life, very few people would choose to be overworked, undervalued, or in a toxic work environment. Spending hours on needless paperwork and redundant processes doesn't top the list either. When life is short, people don't want to spend it doing purposeless work where they don't feel appreciated. So they voted with their feet and left, leading to the Great Resignation and leaving companies in all industries scrambling for talent.[3]

CAREGIVER EXODUS

The great news for workers seeking meaning and purpose is that healthcare's got it! The bad news is that the work is also extremely demanding and carries risks: exposure to disease and violence, inflexible schedules, and intense regulation. As a result, many workers are opting out.

Throughout the pandemic, clinicians were deciding to retire early to ensure that they still had their health to enjoy a lifetime of savings. Besides retirement, an alarming number of clinicians expressed an intention to leave the healthcare workforce altogether. In 2021, over 117,000 physicians left the healthcare workforce.[4] Over 334,000 clinicians of all types left the workforce. More than a third of nurses reported their intention to leave the field altogether or retire by the end of 2022.[5] Among critical care nurses, 66 percent indicated that their experiences during COVID caused them to consider leaving nursing.[6] It is no wonder that workforce shortages topped the list of healthcare CEOs' major concerns for the first time in 2021.[7]

INFLATION AND UNEMPLOYMENT

Broader market dynamics such as inflation and unemployment also complicate matters. Inflation reached a 40-year high in 2022, jumping over 9 percent. Housing prices have seen a nearly 24 percent increase since late 2019.[8] These economic trends have had a twofold effect on healthcare.

First, organizations suffer financially by having to pay significantly more in supply costs. These organizations also suffered revenue reductions because of forced cancellations of elective surgeries and procedures and further reductions because of short-staffing.[9] Second, caregivers who were facing high inflation along with increased job risks demanded higher salaries and wages, leading to high labor costs for healthcare organizations. Organizations with healthy financial margins were able to increase salaries and offer bonuses and hazard pay, while others had to institute pay cuts. Agencies that offered traveling nurses and other workers were paying lucrative salaries. This led to an escalation in costs to maintain staffing levels, further stretching organizations' ability to provide better salaries for their longer-term or loyal employees.

This was occurring as other industries outside of healthcare were also experiencing labor shortages and offering higher salaries, greater flexibility, and generous benefits to attract talent. There are more open positions nationwide than there are job seekers—at the beginning of 2022, there were 10 open spots for every six people looking for a job.[10] Some job descriptions that used to require a master's degree no longer do. Tired of being a nurse? Do this remote online job from home and make more money. Between 2020 and 2022, 54 percent of workers who left a job in the healthcare and pharmaceutical industry did not return to the same industry.[11]

BURNOUT AND DISTRESS

Unfortunately, burnout among healthcare workers has been a problem for a long time. It is one of the leading causes of people intending to leave their organization or to leave the field altogether. A lot of the research on burnout has identified that work-related factors predominantly explain why burnout occurs. We also know that burnout and distress in healthcare are not the result of a lack of individual resilience. Caregivers in general are extraordinarily resilient, but they are working in challenging systems with heavy demands. And it isn't just clinicians. A study found that nearly 75 percent of surveyed healthcare executives reported feeling burned out during the last six months of 2022,[12] compared to 60 percent in 2018.

We also see alarming rates of depression, anxiety, and suicide among our caregivers. The suicide rate for female physicians is 1.46 times higher than the rate for the same age-adjusted population in other professions.[13] Each year, it is estimated that nearly two full medical school classes of physicians die by suicide. Sadly, 55 percent of physicians report knowing another physician who considered, attempted, or died by suicide.[14] These are people who are so committed to the cause—so committed to their patients—that they'll literally work themselves to death. Just replacing the physicians we lose to suicide every year takes a minimum of 4,800 years' worth of education and training, not to mention the knowledge and skills gained through experience.

AGING OF THE POPULATION

As if this wasn't scary enough, one more major trend is straining the human margin: we are getting older.

The aging of the population has been a concern in the healthcare industry for some time. As people age, their needs for healthcare tend to increase. A society can support this as long as it has enough younger caregivers to meet the demand. The challenge in the United States is that the baby boomer generation represents one of the largest demographic groups, with younger groups making up a smaller proportion of the population. As the general population ages and requires more care, the aging caregiver workforce becomes less available to provide it.

In 2020, the median age of a nurse in the United States was 52; in 2022 this number had decreased to 46, largely as a result of older nurses leaving the workforce.[15] This leaves fewer hands to manage the work, and it also results in a loss of years of experience at the bedside and a decline in older mentors for newer nurses.

CHANGING WORK EXPECTATIONS

With new generations entering the workforce, expectations about work are changing. First of all, people are prioritizing flexibility, particularly women and people with caregiving responsibilities.[11] The majority of the nursing workforce is female, and healthcare has a large population of female workers in all roles. Women leaders are 1.5 times more likely than men to leave their jobs to gain more flexibility in their roles, and for organizations that have a greater commitment to diversity, equity, and inclusion.[16]

Employees are also prioritizing employers that they believe care about and support their well-being, with 81 percent of workers listing this as an important consideration for future jobs.[17] Across industries, the majority of workers who left their jobs found themselves in an improved environment with more pay, better advancement opportunities, more flexibility, and a better balance between work and home.[3]

CONCLUSION

While many leaders are deeply committed to creating great experiences for their teams, the external environment continues to add new pressures and challenges. We don't have as much control over what happens outside our walls. These larger industry forces give us a greater sense of why things have gotten harder and remind us of the urgency of tending to the human margin. Everything we do today to care for our people helps set us up to weather the challenges ahead.

REFERENCES

1. Matthews, M. D. 2020. "Mortality Salience During a Pandemic." *Psychology Today*. Published September 4. http://psychologytoday.com/us/blog/head-strong/202009/mortality-salience-during-pandemic.

2. Hu, J., W. He, and K. Zhou. 2020. "The Mind, the Heart, and the Leader in Times of Crisis: How and When COVID-19-Triggered Mortality Salience Relates to State Anxiety, Job Engagement, and Prosocial Behavior." *Journal of Applied Psychology* 105(11): 1218–33.

3. Parker, K., and J. M. Horowitz. 2022. "Majority of Workers Who Quit a Job in 2021 Cite Low Pay, No Opportunities for Advancement, Feeling Disrespected." Pew Research Center. Published March 9. http://pewresearch.org/short-reads/2022/03/09/majority-of-workers-who-quit-a-job-in-2021-cite-low-pay-no-opportunities-for-advancement-feeling-disrespected.

4. Popowitz, E., T. Bellemare, and M. Tieche. 2022. "Addressing the Healthcare Staffing Shortage." Definitive Healthcare. Published October. http://definitivehc.com/sites/default/files/resources/pdfs/Addressing-the_healthcare-staffing-shortage.pdf.

5. Incredible Health. 2022. "Study: 34% of Nurses Plan to Leave Their Current Role by the End of 2022." Published

March 16. http://incrediblehealth.com/blog/nursing-report
-covid-19-2022.

6. American Association of Critical-Care Nurses. 2021. "Hear
    Us Out Campaign Reports Nurses' COVID-19 Reality."
    Published September 21. http://aacn.org/newsroom/hear
    -us-out-campaign-reports-nurses-covid-19-reality.

7. American College of Healthcare Executives. 2022. "Top
    Issues Confronting Hospitals in 2022." Accessed August
    27, 2023. http://ache.org/learning-center/research/about
    -the-field/top-issues-confronting-hospitals/top-issues
    -confronting-hospitals-in-2022.

8. Mondragon, J. A., and J. Wieland. 2022. "Housing Demand
    and Remote Work." National Bureau of Economic Research.
    Published May. https://www.nber.org/papers/w30041.

9. Weise, K., M. Baker, and N. Bogel-Burroughs. 2020. "The
    Coronavirus Is Forcing Hospitals to Cancel Surgeries."
    New York Times. Published March 14. https://www.nytimes
    .com/2020/03/14/us/coronavirus-covid-surgeries-canceled
    .html.

10. Liu, J. 2022. "There Are More than 11 Million Open Jobs in
    America Right Now—and Workers Have the Upper Hand."
    CNBC. Published March 10. http://cnbc.com/2022/03/10
    /there-are-more-than-11-million-open-jobs-in-america-right
    -now.html.

11. De Smet, A., B. Dowling, B. Hancock, and B. Schaninger.
    2022. "The Great Attrition Is Making Hiring Harder. Are
    You Searching the Right Talent Pools?" McKinsey Quarterly.
    Published July. http://mckinsey.com/~/media/mckinsey
    /business%20functions/people%20and%20organizational
    %20performance/our%20insights/the%20great%20
    attrition%20is%20making%20hiring%20harder%20are%20
    you%20searching%20the%20right%20talent%20pools/the
    -great-attrition-is-making-hiring-harder-vf.pdf.

12. Mensik, H. 2022. "Healthcare Executives Also Experiencing Burnout: Survey." Healthcare Dive. Published December 7. http://healthcaredive.com/news/healthcare-executive-CEO-burnout-COVID-pandemic/638195.

13. Duarte, D., M. M. El-Hagrassy, T. Castro e Couto, W. Gurgel, F. Fregni, and H. Correa. 2020. "Male and Female Physician Suicidality: A Systematic Review and Meta-analysis." *JAMA Psychiatry* 77(6): 587–97.

14. The Physicians Foundation. 2021. "New Survey Reveals 55% of Physicians Know a Physician Who Considered, Attempted or Died by Suicide." Published June. http://physiciansfoundation.org/new-survey-reveals-55-of-physicians-know-a-physician-who-considered-attempted-or-died-by-suicide.

15. National Council of State Boards of Nursing. 2022. "National Nursing Workforce Study." Accessed August 31, 2023. http://ncsbn.org/research/recent-research/workforce.page.

16. Lean In. 2022. "Women in the Workplace: 2022." Accessed August 27, 2023. https://leanin.org/women-in-the-workplace/2022/the-state-of-the-pipeline

17. American Psychological Association. 2022. "Workers Appreciate and Seek Mental Health Support in the Workplace." Accessed August 27, 2023. http://apa.org/pubs/reports/work-well-being/2022-mental-health-support.

CHAPTER 3

The Research

MANY EXTERNAL FACTORS are leading to shortages of healthcare workers across the country, and these aren't letting up anytime soon. As a result, staffing shortages are one of the greatest challenges for healthcare organizations today. As people leave the healthcare workforce altogether, we cannot easily or quickly train new replacements. Unlike other industries that rely heavily on human capital, such as food service or hospitality, in healthcare it takes many years to train a clinician to enter the workforce.

The American College of Healthcare Executives (ACHE) annually releases a list of top concerns of healthcare executives. For 16 years, financial pressures topped the list. Now, beginning with the 2021 survey, workforce has taken the top spot.[1] This is not a problem that will resolve quickly, and the struggle to recruit and retain employees will remain a challenge.

So how do we get them, and how do we keep them? Let's see what the research says.

HOW TO KEEP THEM HERE

The most important method of alleviating workforce shortages is to keep the talent you have. This is critically important for many reasons. First of all, when an experienced employee is replaced with a new employee, there is a huge loss in institutional knowledge. Does the new employee know how the mission, vision, and values were created? Do they remember failed projects and lessons learned? Do they have the relationships needed to collaborate across institutional boundaries? All of this takes time for a new employee to develop and build.

Second, there is a loss of productivity. At some point, every new employee needs to learn how to set up their benefits and where the printer is located. This learning process takes time away from other more productive tasks. Many clinicians may need time to develop a base of patients, with whom relationships are critically important for ensuring that patient volumes remain intact. It takes a while for new clinicians to build a referral network and a reputation in the community. When accounting for recruitment costs and lost billing and productivity, the estimated cost of replacing one physician is up to $1.2 million.[2] Other industries estimate that replacing an employee typically costs one-half to two times their annual salary.[3]

A large study looking at 1.4 million employee reviews across multiple industries provides valuable insights into why workers leave. Researchers looked at how employees described their employers and what themes predicted whether they actually left the organization.[4] What they found was that toxic corporate culture was over 10 times more likely to predict turnover than compensation (see exhibit 3.1). Ten times!

Compensation needs to be adequate, but it will never get you from job dissatisfaction to job satisfaction.[5] In our research, we looked at various factors that may help explain why healthcare workers plan to leave, including financial strain, stressors outside of work, meaningful work, and individual resilience. Exhibit 3.2 lists the top 10 drivers of turnover intention identified by our research.

Other large studies have found generally similar results.[7,8] A study of 410,000 caregivers by Press Ganey found that a culture

Exhibit 3.1. Factors That Predict Turnover

Driver of attrition	Relative likelihood of predicting turnover (compared to compensation)	Healthcare example
Toxic corporate culture	10.4x	Gossip, lack of fairness, discrimination at work, abusive leadership
Job insecurity and reorganization	3.5x	Furloughs, layoffs, pay reductions
High levels of innovation	3.2x	Health systems that have an academic mission or research mandate or are transitioning to value-based care models
Failure to recognize employee performance	2.9x	Employees feeling unappreciated for the risks they encounter or the effort they put in
Poor response to COVID-19	1.8x	Lack of access to personal protective equipment (PPE), inequitable distribution of resources, low leader visibility

Source: Adapted from Sull, Sull, and Zweig (2022).[4]

committed to quality and patient-centered care, an ability to make good use of their skills, and an inclusive organizational culture were among the top predictors of whether caregivers wanted to stay with the organization.

What do these combined results tell us?

Exhibit 3.2. The Top 10 Drivers of Turnover Intention

Rank	Predictors of Turnover Intention
1	Burnout
2	Low trust in senior leadership
3	Low perceived organizational support
4	Low sense of belonging
5	Low sense of recognition
6	Feeling that pay is inadequate
7	Unavailability of resources
8	Moral distress
9	Low sense of meaning in work
10	Disrespectful treatment

Source: Meese et al. (2023).[6]

- **It is not necessarily the money.** People may say they are leaving for the money, but it may not be the money. Inadequate pay was on the list of turnover drivers, but it ranked sixth, below many other work-culture characteristics. Reports of financial strain were not statistically significant in the model, meaning that a lack of money in general did not contribute to the intention to leave. When people say, "It is the money," they might actually mean, "You don't pay me enough to put up with this bad work environment." In fact, Gallup's research has found that it takes a 20 percent increase in pay to attract a worker away from a manager who engages them but almost nothing to lure a disengaged employee.[3]
- **Leadership matters at every level.** Trust, culture, and leadership cannot be fully delegated to the front line. There has long been a way of thinking that people don't leave bad organizations—they leave bad managers. Interactions with one's immediate supervisor are critically

important, but the research also highlights the crucial role of senior leaders. Certainly, many of the elements listed in exhibit 3.2—a sense of belonging, respectful treatment, and recognition—are directly influenced by frontline leaders and direct supervisors. However, higher on the list are broader feelings that *senior* leadership is trustworthy and the organization as a whole cares about and values the employee. Similarly, the Department of Veterans Affairs' annual employee survey found that belief in the honesty of senior leaders was among the top five factors for employee engagement.[9] These sentiments reflect a desire to know that whoever is "up there" in the organization is looking out for me and has my best interest at heart. If I don't believe that, then I know that regardless of how good my manager is, I am ultimately not safe here.

- **People want to do their best work.** People want to give their best to their work and to patients, and they want to have the resources and support to do so. Not having the resources to do the right thing or to deliver great care can also cause moral distress.

- **Burnout is still a problem.** Burnout remains a critical issue. The data show that burned-out employees are most likely to leave. This is particularly important in healthcare. Emotional exhaustion is a core component of burnout, and the work of healthcare is inherently emotionally exhausting. If the emotional bank account is empty, the work is nearly impossible to do.

HOW TO KEEP THEM WELL

Just having people stay in the organization is not enough. We want them to be able to do their best work while they are there. Therefore, we have to figure out not only how to keep them from running out the door but also how to keep them well.

Addressing the psychological well-being of our caregivers is not only the right thing to do; it is also crucial if we want them to stay with our organizations. Employees now show a strong preference for employers that support their mental health.[10] Having resources and programs in place for employees is critical, but perhaps more critical is preventing them from experiencing burnout in the first place.

The research on chronic stress and its effects on our brains is quite scary. It can lead to changes in the structure and functioning of our brains, which we will discuss further in the well-being chapter. This gives us a deeper sense of the critical importance of creating environments where our caregivers are not existing in chronically, unrelentingly stressful situations.

Is that goal even possible? Isn't healthcare work stressful by definition? We are dealing with death on a daily basis.

A deeper dive into what contributes to distress among caregivers can give us some clues. It wasn't at all what we expected to find.

In 2020, we researched overall distress in a large caregiver population. We looked at over 40 unique stressors for healthcare workers—ranging from heavy workloads and lack of PPE to death of a loved one, divorce, and lack of childcare—to see which ones were most likely to explain their distress. It was a traumatic time for clinicians and for the leaders who were trying hard to provide relief to their teams but falling short.

The top work-related stressors across groups were fear of COVID infection, reduced income, rapid changes in workflow, increased responsibilities, fear of job loss, and inadequate access to PPE. Most people *said* that those things were causing their distress. That is the part we expected. What we didn't expect was that the list was very different when we analyzed the data to see what factors were statistically explaining overall distress scores.

Exhibit 3.3 shows the top 10 factors that statistically predicted overall distress.

We were completely shocked not to see the COVID-related factors at the top of the list. We were even more shocked that personal factors such as childcare stress, job insecurity, and death of a loved

Exhibit 3.3. The Top 10 Predictors of Distress

2020	2022
1. Heavy workload and long hours	1. Low job satisfaction
2. Increased job demands and responsibilities	2. Post-traumatic stress symptoms because of events between 2020 and 2022
3. Moral distress	3. Lack of autonomy
4. Lack of perceived organizational support	4. Heavy workload or job responsibilities
5. Lack of autonomy	5. Moral distress
6. Perceived inequity of pay cut	6. Unwilling to recommend the organization to a friend or colleague
7. Loneliness and social isolation	7. Lack of recognition
8. High risk of COVID-19 exposure	8. Compassion fatigue
9. Lower resilience	9. Low sense of belonging
10. Fear of infecting family with COVID-19	10. Long hours

Source: Meese et al. (2021).[11,12]

one didn't make the list. It was the *work*. It was the heavy workload, the feeling that their organization didn't support them, and the feeling that they couldn't do the right thing. Lack of control and perceptions of inequity came next. COVID-specific factors didn't make the list until number eight. In 2022, durable work-related factors continued to top the list.

Ultimately, the factors that led to higher distress during the pandemic were similar to factors identified before and after it (such as workload, organizational support, fairness, and recognition). The great news is we can do something about those stressors—we have some control, even when other things feel out of control.

It is also important to note that job satisfaction is the top predictor of overall well-being. This is quite shocking. Of all the things in our lives, at home and at work, job satisfaction is the top factor that explains our overall well-being. If you aren't satisfied at work, you are far less likely to be well in general. This really highlights the importance of creating healthy work where people can flourish.

HOW TO GET NEW HUMANS

It is important to keep our people and keep them well, but inevitably we will also need to recruit new people into the organization. One of the most important sources of recruitment is your current employee base. You want them to tell their friends, family, and professional network to come and join the work. What makes people want to tell their friends to come work in the organization? Net Promoter Score (NPS) asks, "On a scale of 1 to 10, how likely are you to recommend working in the organization to a friend or acquaintance?" The answer tells us two things: (1) How successful will we be at recruiting? (2) Do employees feel proud to work here?[13]

The factors that influence NPS are slightly different from those that predict turnover. The following elements were ranked according to how strongly they were associated with an improved NPS and a higher likelihood to recommend the organization:

1. Perceived organizational support
2. Trust in senior leadership
3. Resource availability
4. Sense of recognition
5. Sense of belonging
6. Trust in supervisor
7. Respect

8. Autonomy
9. Low employee burnout
10. Lack of moral distress

Again, the two most important factors concern broad, organizational matters: *Does the organization care about and support me, and do I trust the people at the top?*

WHAT THIS MEANS

The great news is that many of the factors that show up again and again can be addressed. What a relief! The greater news is that addressing many of these elements is also free. In a time of financial strain within many organizations, "free" is really good. The best news is that every individual on the healthcare team can have a role in making improvements in many of these areas. We don't need to have a certain title or wait for the entire organization to change—we can do things right now to make it better.

We have distilled these findings to focus on a few key areas that people at all levels of leadership can influence and that are likely to have the greatest effect on recruitment, retention, and well-being. We will explore these areas in the following chapters and offer practical tips and techniques you can use to move the needle from wherever you sit.

REFERENCES

1. American College of Healthcare Executives (ACHE). 2023. "Top Issues Confronting Hospitals." Accessed August 30. http://ache.org/learning-center/research/about-the-field /top-issues-confronting-hospitals/top-issues-confronting -hospitals-in-2022.

2. Berg, S. 2018. "How Much Physician Burnout Is Costing Your Organization." American Medical Association. Published October 11. http://ama-assn.org/practice-management /physician-health/how-much-physician-burnout-costing-your -organization.

3. Gandhi, V., and J. Robison. 2021. "The 'Great Resignation' Is Really the 'Great Discontent.'" Gallup. Published July 22. https://www.gallup.com/workplace/351545/great-resignation -really-great-discontent.aspx.

4. Sull, D., C. Sull, and B. Zweig. 2022. "Toxic Culture Is Driving the Great Resignation." *MIT Sloan Management Review* 63(2): 1–9.

5. Herzberg, F., B. Mausner, and B. B. Snyderman. 2011. *The Motivation to Work*. Abingdon, UK: Transaction.

6. Meese, K. A., L. Boitet, A. Gorman, N. Patel, L. Nassetta, and D. A. Rogers. 2023. "Don't Go: Examining the Relationships Between Purpose, Work Environment and Turnover Intention Across the Entire Healthcare Team." Dublin: European Academy of Management annual meeting.

7. Linzer, M., J. O. Jin, P. Shah, M. Stillman, R. Brown, S. Poplau, N. Nankivil, K. Cappelucci, and C. A. Sinsky. "Trends in Clinician Burnout with Associated Mitigating and Aggravating Factors During the COVID-19 Pandemic." *JAMA Health Forum* 3(11): e224163.

8. Ryan, P. T., and T. H. Lee. 2023. "What Makes Health Care Workers Stay in Their Jobs?" *Harvard Business Review*. Published March 2. http://hbr.org/2023/03/what-makes-health -care-workers-stay-in-their-jobs.

9. VHA National Center for Organization Development. 2018. "2018 VA All Employee Survey Responses for Items from the OPM Federal Employee Viewpoint Survey." US Department

of Veterans Affairs. Updated March 20, 2023. http://datahub
.va.gov/dataset/AES-2018-FEVS-Percents/isnh-negm.

10. De Smet, A., B. Dowling, B. Hancock, and B. Schaninger.
2022 "The Great Attrition Is Making Hiring Harder. Are You
Searching the Right Talent Pools?" *McKinsey Quarterly*. Published July 13. http://mckinsey.com/capabilities/people-and
-organizational-performance/our-insights/the-great-attrition
-is-making-hiring-harder-are-you-searching-the-right-talent
-pools.

11. Meese, K. A., A. Colón-López, J. A. Singh, G. A. Burkholder,
and D. A. Rogers. 2021. "Healthcare Is a Team Sport: Stress,
Resilience, and Correlates of Well-Being Among Health System Employees in a Crisis." *Journal of Healthcare Management*
66(4): 304–22.

12. Meese, K. A. Unpublished data. (Details of this work are
provided in the Appendix.)

13. Brown, M. I. 2020. "Comparing the Validity of Net Promoter
and Benchmark Scoring to Other Commonly Used Employee
Engagement Metrics." *Human Resource Development Quarterly* 31(4): 355–70.

CHAPTER 4

Building and Restoring Trust

TRUST IS A critical element of workplace culture. A systematic review of 75 studies on trust found a strong link between trust in leadership and job, team, and organizational performance.[1] As Stephen M. R. Covey says, the presence of trust accelerates everything.[2] The more that people trust each other, the more engaged and willing they are to take risks and the faster they move. Conversely, a lack of trust halts progress.

In general, trust contributes to a healthy and positive work environment marked by open communication, mutual respect, and a commitment to shared values. Your organization becomes a great place to work, one where people can flourish and feel connected to their calling. Word gets around, and soon your organization may find itself attracting the best and brightest talent. All of this works together to improve performance, productivity, and patient outcomes.

Trust makes people more resilient and adaptable. The presence of trust also replenishes those we lead. When times are tough and we go through periods of crisis and disruption, employees who trust us will stick with us. They know we'll make decisions in the organization's and their own best interests.

More than other factors, trust becomes a lens through which all other interactions and experiences are viewed. If trust is present, people tend to have the most generous interpretation of others' actions and intentions. When trust is broken, even the most innocent of actions may be interpreted as dubious, duplicitous, or malicious.

Who has not heard that "people don't leave their job; they leave their boss"? The direct supervisor plays a very important role in retention; however, our own data emphasized the importance of trust in *senior* leadership specifically. Our data showed that trust in senior leadership was important in explaining both whether caregivers planned to leave and whether they would recommend the organization. In fact, trust in senior leadership was the number-two predictor of both turnover intention and willingness to recommend the organization. Trust in one's supervisor also mattered for the net promoter score, but that factor did not even make the top-10 list for turnover intention.[3] We also saw that the levels of trust varied widely across the organization even in areas where employees had the same senior leaders.

These results tell us three important things:

1. Trust really, really matters for recruitment and retention.
2. Trust building isn't something that can be delegated completely to the front line or the direct supervisor.
3. Midlevel leaders have a role in shaping their teams' trust of senior leaders.

We will talk more about how to close the senior leader trust gap later in this chapter. First, though, let's look at how trust manifests in our behaviors.

WHAT TRUST LOOKS LIKE IN ACTION

Trust is built with consistency over time. We can't just decide, "Okay, from now on I'm going to be a trustworthy person." Trustworthiness arises from the consistent demonstration of other traits, such as honesty, integrity, humility, and empathy. It exists in the perception of others. Unfortunately, research shows that distrust tends to be most people's default position.[4] In other words, many people automatically distrust us until we give them a reason not to.

What's more, it is almost impossible to fake trustworthiness. We have to consistently demonstrate to others that we can be trusted. People will sense whether we're faking it. They will intuitively feel that our behavior is a façade.

The good news is that it is possible to genuinely grow into a trustworthy person. Most people who are highly trusted don't necessarily think, "I am building trust." Rather, trust is a by-product of the relationships they build and the behaviors they consistently exhibit. There are some consistent behaviors and strategies to keep in mind for building trust. To help us remember, we developed the acronym **CHORES 1st**.

CHORES 1st for Building Trust

C: Competence and Consistency. Work hard to develop the competence and skills to do the job well. People need to be able to trust that your work is done with excellence. Trust is built with consistency over time. Just having competence doesn't build trust unless you are also able to deliver on your commitments. Develop good boundaries so you don't overextend yourself. Do what you say you are going to do. If you realize that you can't for some reason, let people know as soon as possible. Every interaction is a calculation of increased or diminished trust.

H: Honesty. Be honest, even when it's hard. Face difficult conversations head-on. Have the courage to tell people the truth. Give honest feedback, but do it with humility, kindness, and compassion. Don't avoid hard conversations for short-term comfort or to save face. Also, give people as much information as you can. When they understand the rationale and all the constraints of the environment, they are more likely to arrive at the same logical decisions. It's better to overshare than undershare.

O: Own your mistakes. No one is perfect. When we're willing to admit our mistakes, it helps us connect with people. It also encourages our teams to be honest and speak up without fear of retribution—a critical component of psychological safety. Have the courage to admit when you've made a mistake. Talk to those who were affected by the decision and ask for forgiveness. Ask them what would help avoid the mistake or make it better next time (more on this later in the chapter).

R: Relationship. It is hard to trust somebody you don't know. Think of what you do as relationship building. Don't get so focused on getting things done that you lose sight of building one-on-one personal relationships. Get to know each person as an individual. Assume good intentions on the part of others, and they will extend that courtesy to you. Do this throughout the organization, not just with your team.

E: Expectations. Set clear expectations so that people know what "right" looks like, and be clear on what happens when expectations are not met. Clarifying expectations gives people the information they need to perform at their best. If they know the expectations, they are more likely to understand why and how performance issues will be addressed. Help people meet their goals, and don't shame them when they are struggling. Let people know with words and actions that you are committed to their success. Be flexible; meet people where they are. Personalize your approach. Treat people with respect, particularly if they are struggling with a performance gap.

S: Safety. Psychological safety is the feeling that one can speak up with ideas, questions, concerns, or mistakes without punishment or humiliation. It is one of the most important characteristics of a trust-centered organization. People are more likely to trust you and one another when they feel psychologically safe. Learn to accept hard feedback graciously. Never respond negatively when people bring you news that you'd prefer not to hear.

1st: First show people that you trust them. Trust is a two-way street. People are more likely to trust when they feel trusted. One way to show this trust is to get people involved in decision-making and problem-solving. The more that employees get to share their ideas and perspectives, the greater their buy-in will be. People like knowing that their insights are valued by leaders, and because they are closer to the action, they might be the best people to solve problems anyway.

One way to show that you trust people is to ask them to help solve problems. Asking groups to come up with solutions builds teamwork and achieves better results. When you do ask, be specific. For example, say: "We are struggling with falls. What are your thoughts on how we can be better?" or "We seem to be losing new hires in the first six months. What can we do to reduce these departures?" Show people that it is safe to speak up and to share their ideas and feedback. Create an environment where they can tell you the truth.

Adopting these behaviors doesn't help unless you are out and about with people. Leverage the power of rounding (more on this in chapter 7). When it's done well, rounding is a huge trust builder and relationship strengthener. It is vitally important to demonstrate openness and honesty and to encourage people to share their concerns. It also demonstrates a leader's commitment to truly understanding—and ultimately solving—the challenges people face on the front lines.

Rounding builds the necessary trust for employees to speak up and also makes it more likely that leaders will see things that employees may still be reluctant to share (despite your best efforts). This is how people truly engage in the organization. We are asking people to do hard things and bring us solutions to tough problems. They have to feel the psychological safety to give honest feedback, take risks, float creative ideas, and put themselves on the line for the organization.

In summary: act with integrity, prioritize relationships, and build others up. And if you want people to trust you, strive always to be worthy of that trust.

THE SENIOR LEADERSHIP TRUST GAP

As mentioned earlier, employees have shifted from focusing on front-line bosses to focusing on senior leadership. The presence or absence of trust in senior leaders has a lot to do with whether someone plans to leave their job and whether they're willing to recommend the organization to others.

So what is causing the trust gap? It's not that people in senior leadership are inherently untrustworthy. Most of them are good people trying to do the right thing. Those serving in the C-suite are like most people in healthcare: They want to make a difference. They want to create an organization that does things right.

Senior leaders have huge responsibility and accountability and are pulled in many different directions. Their job is to do the internal work of creating a well-run organization while also responding to external pressures from the community, the political world, the payors, and rapid changes in diseases and technologies.

Helping workers understand that senior leaders want to do a great job is half the battle. The other half is being focused and intentional about closing the trust gap.

HOW CAN WE CLOSE THE TRUST GAP?

First, recognize the existence of the gap and try to understand what causes it. The most critical and obvious element is that leaders act in a trustworthy manner, choosing integrity and genuinely caring for their people. The first step is an honest self-assessment. Are there areas of your behavior that may create a perception of untrustworthiness?

Assuming that leaders are acting with integrity and doing the right thing, other factors may be creating a trust gap.

One factor may be physical distance. Senior leaders may work on different floors or in different buildings, and the size of the organization may make it difficult to be visible on all floors, units, and shifts. When people don't see leaders, it's hard to develop a personal connection with them. It is difficult to trust somebody that you do not know. This leads to emotional distance. Time constraints and demands from many stakeholders further complicate the leader's goal of being visible and accessible.

It's not hard to see why a great divide opens between what senior leaders are doing and what the front line thinks they are doing. And while leaders may not be able to do a lot about the time and space factors, there is one very powerful tool at their disposal: communication.

Most senior leaders *want* to eliminate the gap between themselves and frontline workers, but it is hard to do so. There are lots of people in the middle. Information may be filtered or distorted as it passes through various levels of management, leading to misunderstandings between senior leaders and frontline employees. In other words, there are lots of opportunities for things to go wrong.

Let's say an organization has 5,000 employees. The largest group consists of the frontline and hourly employees. In this hypothetical organization, 10 members are in the C-suite. There are 400 leaders between the 10 in the C-suite and the 4,590 frontline staff. These 400 people are the gap managers. Each day they do one of three things: close the communication and trust gap, keep it the same, or make it worse.

MIDLEVEL LEADERS ARE THE KEY TO CLOSING THE GAP

Midlevel leaders relay your information from senior leadership to lower levels of the organization and are key to aligning messages and sharing them in a way that builds trust rather than erodes it. Make sure midlevel leaders understand how they affect the trust of the frontline team. There is no substitute for experience, and many leaders in healthcare organizations are new to the role or the job and may unknowingly do things that break down trust. Train your midlevel leaders on what builds trust and what tears it down, because their ability to master the fundamentals of trust building is essential to closing the gap.

One of the biggest erosions of trust occurs when employees ask tough questions and leaders don't know how to respond. Not only does the uncertainty around what they're "allowed" to say create a lot of anxiety for the leaders, but it also can make them answer in ways that perpetuate the dreaded "we/they" or "us vs. them" dynamic. *We/they* is a culture killer. It destroys trust, fosters blame and finger-pointing, and weakens the relationships that allow people to work together productively.

In a we/they culture, a manager is happy to say yes to an employee request (and get the win). But if the manager is unsure, they may say, "Let me run this by [senior leaders]." Then, if the manager returns and delivers a no, the employee may thank them for trying—while feeling bad that the manager must work with these senior leaders.

Midlevel leaders can exhibit we/they behaviors at times without even being aware they are doing it. They have not been provided with the needed information to communicate well. They have not been provided with the skill building on how *not* to communicate. Once their reliance on we/they is pointed out, managers quickly realize it is something they don't want to keep doing.

HELPING LEADERS ANSWER TOUGH QUESTIONS

Frontline leaders (those positioned between hourly employees and senior or executive leaders) get asked a lot of questions because employees encounter them most often. They want to be able to answer questions and provide assurance and information. Not knowing the answers to tough questions could lead to we/they scenarios. If these leaders don't know how to answer, they may be reluctant to be out and about among employees or may resort to blaming senior leaders.

Determining which questions are frequently asked and providing suggested ways to respond is invaluable to leaders. This helps prepare them and aligns the organization, as it creates leadership consistency in responding to staff's concerns and questions.

Here's an exercise that organizations find very helpful. Before a meeting with frontline leaders, a request is sent to all attendees that asks them to anonymously fill out a one-question survey: "When you are talking with those you lead, what questions are you hearing?" Then collect the identified questions. Many of the questions are ones that senior leaders can quickly answer. Other questions are consistently heard by managers and supervisors. These questions fall into various categories: staffing, pay, benefits, rumors, hours of operation, the organization's financial condition, equipment, supplies, and so forth.

Next, divide attendees into groups, with each group receiving one question. This is the assignment: "When you hear this question, what is the best way to respond?" At the end of the meeting, the organization takes the work of all the groups and creates a tool kit on frequently heard questions with recommended responses.

This exercise helps those who are currently in leadership roles and is also wonderful for new leaders who come aboard later. It is a safe way to share what frontline leaders are hearing. It also creates consistency in responses and helps the senior leader team become more aware of how to improve communication. Having approved ways to respond to questions greatly reduces leaders' anxiety, and the communication consistency reduces employee anxiety.

Unexpected Questions

Managers often ask, "If someone asks me a question and I don't know the answer, what do I say?" One suggested response is "Let me research this, and I will get back to you with an answer in [an estimated time]." If you find out that it will take more time than you thought, provide an update. Own the response. While it may not be comfortable, there are times when a leader needs to own a tough message. Be honest and transparent and provide the "why" when you can. Even though it's not what people want to hear, it does build trust.

Getting clarity around how to answer tough questions is only one way for managers to avoid we/they patterns and close the trust gap. Another is to take time to recognize and appreciate when senior leadership does things right. By recognizing and acknowledging the accomplishments and efforts of those above and below us, we can set a good example for other employees. While negative gossip can be detrimental, positive gossip (sharing good things about others) has individual and organizational benefits.[5]

All that said, no leader at any level is perfect. We all make mistakes from time to time. That's why we need to make sure we are willing and able to own our mistakes, ask for forgiveness, and restore trust once it's broken.

THE SCIENCE OF REPAIR

What if we normalized forgiveness at work: both asking for it and giving it?

We would be remiss in discussing trust without also discussing forgiveness. When trust is broken, some forgiveness is necessary for repair. Forgiveness is important not only for working towards restoring trust but also for bringing benefits to the forgiver. Over 128 research studies show a consistent relationship between forgiveness and better physical health.[6] The positive relationship between forgiveness and psychological health is even stronger,[7] including lower anxiety, reduced depression and post-traumatic stress disorder, and even a restored sense of humanness.[8] A study of over 54,000 nurses found that forgiveness was related to improved psychological well-being and social integration over time.[9] Simply put, forgiving is good for our minds and bodies.

It is unlikely that any leader who has been in the role for a while has no need of forgiveness for at least *something*. Healthcare is filled with many unknowns, rapidly changing information, impossible trade-offs and decisions, morally distressing situations, a vanishing workforce, and extreme resource constraints. These conditions can lead to decisions that in retrospect may have caused unintentional harm. Because leaders are themselves at risk for high degrees of psychological distress and fear during crises, their brains are not always optimized for ideal decision-making. Even if they were, difficult trade-offs often have to be made. Our data clearly show that in both clinical and nonclinical settings, those with leadership or supervisory roles had higher distress during a time of crisis than those without those roles. The burden of leadership is heavy, and most leaders want to do the right thing.

Despite the impossibility of a situation, damage to trust still may occur. Forgiveness provides an antidote. It is extremely powerful.

One of the best ways to resolve a situation and gain forgiveness is to apologize. Most people want to forgive. We want to be able to make peace and move on. We want to believe in our leaders, our colleagues, and our organizations. So when we do apologize and receive forgiveness, we open the door to stronger and better relationships.

Restorative justice is a process that seeks to support reconciliation between the victim and the offender. It is used in various ways in schools and criminal justice. According to the Restorative Justice Exchange, "Restorative justice is a response to wrongdoing that prioritizes repairing harm and recognizes that maintaining positive relationships with others is a core human need."[10] It is a model that seeks to repair and restore rather than to punish.

Restorative justice involves three phases:

1. **Encounter**—Once the perpetrator has acknowledged wrongdoing, the perpetrator and the victim have a facilitated meeting to talk, where victims are able to express what would repair the harm.

2. **Repair**—This phase addresses the victim's need for healing and closure and the offender's need to make amends.
3. **Transform**—This phase allows the restored victim and the offender to pinpoint root causes of the harm and identify systemic issues and solutions to prevent future harm.[10]

Before these phases start, it is important that the offender admits to wrongdoing. This is where things frequently break down in the repair process. Because of our desire to avoid embarrassment or shame or our fear of the ramifications of owning our mistakes, we often avoid taking responsibility for those mistakes. We find alternate explanations for why we couldn't have acted any other way. Even if the harm was completely unintentional or if there were no options other than the difficult choice that helped one group at the expense of another, we can still apologize for the harm it caused.

Asking for forgiveness is critical not only for repairing trust; forgiveness is critical also for organizational performance. Forgiveness of leaders is associated with improved job satisfaction,[11] which is an important deterrent for turnover. Forgiveness can also improve innovation, organizational performance, and employee productivity.[12,13] Asking for forgiveness doesn't just benefit employees and the organization; it benefits the person making the apology too. Apologizing is linked with improved psychological well-being and emotional health.[14]

Good relationships build trust, and trust builds good relationships. Not only does this translate into operational efficiency, but it also has a huge impact on our well-being and helps create a place where people want to be.

REFERENCES

1. Guinot, J., and R. Chiva. 2019. "Vertical Trust Within Organizations and Performance: A Systematic Review." *Human Resource Development Review* 18(2): 196–227.

2. Covey, S. R., and R. R. Merrill. 2006. *The Speed of Trust: The One Thing That Changes Everything*. New York: Simon and Schuster.

3. Meese, K. A., L. Boitet, A. Gorman, N. Patel, L. Nassetta, and D. A. Rogers. 2023. "Don't Go: Examining the Relationships Between Purpose, Work Environment and Turnover Intention Across the Entire Healthcare Team." Dublin: European Academy of Management annual meeting.

4. Edelman. 2022. *Edelman Trust Barometer 2022: The Trust 10*. Published January 19. http://edelman.com/sites/g/files/aatuss191/files/2022-01/Trust%2022_Top10.pdf.

5. Wax, A., W. A. Rodriguez, and R. Asencio. 2022. "Spilling Tea at the Water Cooler: A Meta-analysis of the Literature on Workplace Gossip." *Organizational Psychology Review* 12(4): 453–506.

6. Lee, Y.-R., and R. D. Enright. 2019. "A Meta-analysis of the Association Between Forgiveness of Others and Physical Health." *Psychology & Health* 34(5): 626–43.

7. Rasmussen, K. R., M. Stackhouse, S. D. Boon, K. Comstock, and R. Ross. 2019. "Meta-analytic Connections Between Forgiveness and Health: The Moderating Effects of Forgiveness-Related Distinctions." *Psychology & Health* 34(5): 515–34.

8. Schumann, K., and G. M. Walton. 2021. "Rehumanizing the Self After Victimization: The Roles of Forgiveness Versus Revenge." *Journal of Personality and Social Psychology*. Published June 17. http://dx.doi.org/10.1037/pspi0000367.

9. Long, K. N., E. L. Worthington Jr., T. J. VanderWeele, and Y. Chen. 2020. "Forgiveness of Others and Subsequent Health and Well-Being in Mid-life: A Longitudinal Study on Female Nurses." *BMC Psychology* 8(104): 1–11.

10. Restorative Justice Exchange. 2023. "Three Core Elements of Restorative Justice." Accessed September 1. http://restorativejustice.org/what-is-restorative-justice/three-core-elements-of-restorative-justice.

11. Radulovic, A. B., G. Thomas, O. Epitropaki, and A. Legood. 2019. "Forgiveness in Leader–Member Exchange Relationships: Mediating and Moderating Mechanisms." *Journal of Occupational and Organizational Psychology* 92(3): 498–534.

12. Domínguez-Escrig, E., F. F. M. Broch, R. C. Gómez, and R. L. Alcamí. 2022. "Improving Performance Through Leaders' Forgiveness: The Mediating Role of Radical Innovation." *Personnel Review* 51(1): 4–20.

13. Toussaint, L., E. L. Worthington Jr., D. R. Van Tongeren, J. Hook, J. W. Berry, V. A. Shivy, A. J. Miller, and D. E. Davis. 2018. "Forgiveness Working: Forgiveness, Health, and Productivity in the Workplace." *American Journal of Health Promotion* 32(1): 59–67.

14. Byrne, A., J. Barling, and K. E. Dupré. 2014. "Leader Apologies and Employee and Leader Well-Being." *Journal of Business Ethics* 121(1): 91–106.

CHAPTER 5

Belonging

An important element of building trust is creating an environment where everyone can feel that they belong. If we feel devalued or excluded in our work environment, it is hard to trust the people around us.

Creating a sense of belonging isn't just about doing the right thing. Creating an environment where people feel like they belong is also good for business. The research is clear that when people with different voices, perspectives, and backgrounds have a seat and a voice at the table, performance improves.[1] This is becoming more important than ever in the battle for talent. New job reports on what workers are looking for at work show that people are choosing work environments that they believe support inclusion and belonging.[2,3]

In our own research on caregivers, a sense of belonging was associated with better overall well-being and an intention to stay in the organization and promote it to others. Fostering a sense of belonging is not just about creating a great environment for current caregivers but also about attracting, hiring, and retaining the best talent in the industry to be a part of your organization or team. It is also about keeping them well and able to give their best to patients and to one another.

Not belonging can be very lonely, and we spend too much time at work to feel lonely there. Loneliness has a profound effect on physical health and mental well-being. A large study found that chronic loneliness has a similar effect on your health and longevity as smoking about 15 cigarettes per day.[45] We are not encouraging you to pick up a new smoking habit. But what this research tells us is that it would essentially be healthier to find a friend and smoke 14 cigarettes a day together than to be chronically lonely.

We don't want to create organizations where everybody feels like they must look and act the same way to belong. We want to create organizations where our shared values are lived out and protected so that everyone can belong as long as we have those values in common. Some organizations do a really good job of communicating these shared values and even screening for adoption of them during the hiring process. That gives us a greater chance of having people in our organizations and teams who can unite around common ideals. In healthcare, we have a great advantage that many of us are in the industry because we want to bring healing and health to patients, whether we work in the supply chain or at the bedside.

ELEMENTS OF BELONGING

The research literature suggests that several key elements contribute to a sense of belonging.

- **Competencies:** This is a person's ability to engage in behaviors that foster social connection. An employee who lacks these skills may benefit from coaching and development. These behaviors include understanding social cues, emotional regulation, and an ability to engage in conversation with others.
- **Opportunities to belong:** This is the availability of people, time, and places for employees to connect. These opportunities may include gathering in a physical office location or planning regular meetings or events at which people can connect. Employers may also create affinity

groups that like-minded individuals can use to connect within the organization.

- **Motivation:** This is a person's intrinsic desire to belong and connect with others. Most people have at least some motivation to belong at work, though the extent of the need varies.[6]
- **Perceptions:** Even if a person has the skills, opportunities, and motivation to belong, they can still have a perception that they just don't fit in. This can be heavily influenced by past experiences or by the biases and actions of others.

IN-GROUPS AND OUT-GROUPS

It is also important to note that we can't feel that we belong if we also feel "less-than" or "other" because of some element of our personal history, experiences, background, appearance, or social standing. Unfortunately, this often happens in reality (more on this in chapter 8).

Humans tend to think highly of ourselves, so we often want to hire and promote a bunch of people just like us. Our tendency is for "birds of a feather to flock together." One problem is that homogeneous teams typically underperform on most tasks compared to diverse teams, though sometimes the decision-making processes on diverse teams come with more conflict. The degree of improved performance is influenced by whether the team's diversity is managed well. When a new person joins an organization or team, they tend to be categorized into the "in-group" or the "out-group."[7,8] This usually happens subconsciously.

In-group selection may include people who graduated from a certain school, look a certain way, or even view work similarly (e.g., "In *our* department we work hard and play hard!"). It could be based on gender, parental status, wardrobe, the football team you root for, or whether you initiate a hangout after work. These in-group members typically get more engagement, more mentoring and coaching from the leaders, and more opportunities for growth and high-profile exposures. There is a pretty good chance you view somebody as part of the in-group if you think, "That person really looks like a leader" or "We need to hire more people like them."

The out-group is usually characterized by "not really fitting in here." This categorization usually happens quickly and unconsciously and often has less to do with competence than with external characteristics and the preferences of the leader. This is a big problem, because the in-group usually outperforms the out-group as a result of the extra support they get. Once somebody is categorized into the out-group, they get fewer resources and their performance suffers, leading to a self-fulfilling prophecy. This arrangement makes a big difference in terms of the relational connections needed for success.

BELONGING AT THE CENTER

A sense of belonging is central to all other conditions needed for employees to flourish and for organizations to maximize the human margin. Belonging and engagement go hand in hand.

A sense of belonging is a powerful intrinsic motivator. *Intrinsic* describes a characteristic that is essential to something's nature. When we are intrinsically motivated, we don't do things to be recognized for the action. We participate because of the emotions it brings us: joy, fulfillment, and a sense of purpose. We do it because we think, "I belong here." Intrinsic motivation drives us to achieve self-awareness and self-improvement. It is the internal emotion that adds to our emotional bank account. *Extrinsic* motivators are rewards that come not from within but from outside ourselves. These can be compensation, promotions, awards, and so forth. There is nothing wrong with extrinsic motivators, but building a sense of belonging will get more results over the long term than extrinsic rewards alone.

WHAT CAN YOU DO TO GIVE PEOPLE A SENSE OF BELONGING?

Entire books have been written on belonging. It is a complex subject. It is helpful to stay away from words like "simple" and "easy" as well as terms like "little things." If creating a culture of belonging with all its accompanying benefits were simple or easy, this book would not be needed. And in leadership there are no little things. Everything we do or say has an impact.

- **Get intentional.** First, understand that creating a sense of belonging doesn't just happen. When we get intentional about creating it, we can see the endless opportunities to make people feel like they are part of the team.
- **Focus on mission, vision, and values.** It may also help to do a deep dive into your organization's mission, vision, and values. It is more likely that by focusing on these shared values, you can bring a diverse team together around these values and create a deeper sense of belonging. It is also important for making sure that new hires into the organization align with your values. By screening new employees for values alignment on the way in, you maximize the chance that they will be able to experience a sense of belonging. It's vital that the new hire gets a feel for your culture early on. This will help them fit in more quickly so they can experience that crucial sense of belonging that makes them want to stay and sets them up to succeed long-term.
- **Start early.** In fact, it is important to start building belonging well before the employee is hired and starts the job: during the interview process, during preboarding (that window between accepting the job and officially starting work), and during onboarding, which is the time frame when people feel most vulnerable.

We can build belonging by involving potential coworkers in the selection process. This actually creates a sense of belonging for both parties. The applicant gets to know their future coworkers, and the coworkers get input into selection. A cautionary note is to be mindful of the tendency to select those who remind us of ourselves.

We now know that accepting a job and showing up for it are two different actions. The earlier we can create that sense of belonging, the more likely a new hire is to follow through. Even after the job has been accepted, we still need to "court" the candidate.

Consider the following example from TriHealth in Cincinnati, Ohio. Department director Joi Lindlau keeps in touch with every new hire before they even start the job. A few days before the actual start date, the new hire receives a message from her. It shows which parking lot to park in (during the interview process the person parks in a different spot, and TriHealth has a big campus) and which entrance to use. She even includes a photo of the door they will enter. Joi includes a reminder to the new hire to wear their name badge and assures them that she will meet them at the door on the first day. This is a good way to stay connected with the new hire. It shows caring and reduces anxiety.

There are other ways to create belonging during the preboarding session. For example, you might send a welcome video from the team. Employees often question whether they have made the right decision when selecting an employer. Let them know that they have indeed made the right decision and are in the right place.

A new hire will be comparing their "insides" (how they feel) with the "outsides" (how other people appear) of more experienced employees. This creates that "less-than" feeling and generates thoughts such as "I don't belong." The excitement of a new job can diminish quickly. There's a new boss and new teammates. There can also be different technology, different processes, and so forth. Tasks take longer to achieve, and the individual feels they are not making it.

Another effective way to address this feeling is to have the more experienced staff meet with the new hire to share how they felt those first days. Many organizations commingle employees who are new to their roles and the organization with experienced people who are only new to the organization. For example, during nurse orientation, new graduates and experienced nurses who are just new to the organization attend the same general nurse orientation. For experienced nurses, the challenge is to show interest in items that may be very routine. New graduates will be cautious to speak up and may be intimidated by the experienced nurses. Some of the experienced nurses may have forgotten how they felt as new grads.

Here is a solution that helps everyone. At the beginning of the session, ask each experienced nurse to share how they felt when they started their first job. You will feel the mood in the room shift. It brings the experienced nurses back to their start. Brand-new grads think, "You felt like this too, and look how well you have done!" Connections will be built. It creates belonging.

That is just one example of how you can take straightforward action to foster a sense of belonging among your team members. Other strategies include the following:

- **Say it.** Tell your people that they belong on the team. You might say, "I am so glad you are here. You are just what our team needs" or "I love the creativity you bring to this team."
- **Get intentional about building relationships with employees.** Get to know them by showing an interest in both their personal lives and their professional growth.
- **Encourage open communication.** The heart of belonging centers around being heard, understood, and valued. By creating an environment where employees feel comfortable sharing their ideas and concerns, leaders can demonstrate that they value their employees' input and engagement.

- **Be an accessible leader.** Sometimes rigid structures get in the way of people feeling that they can come to you. Break down these barriers by letting them know that your door is always open and that you are willing to hear hard things.
- **Make sure employees understand what training and development will look like.** New hires (and especially young people) want to be assured that they'll grow and progress in your company. Let them know up-front that you take this seriously. Inform them that you'll create an individualized development plan for each employee and review it no less frequently than every month. When you tell employees up-front that you plan to invest in them, it not only relieves anxiety but also helps them feel cared for. That's an important part of belonging.
- **Provide frequent (and early) feedback and coaching.** This relieves anxiety and lets employees know how they are doing. It also lets them know you are invested in them and that they are important parts of the team.
- **Be on the lookout for biases.** Because we tend to gravitate toward people like ourselves, it is easy to develop blind spots and biases in how we treat and include others. Be watchful for the formation of in-groups. What unspoken features tend to give somebody a better chance of being in an in-group? Be proactive in giving everyone support, attention, and the chance to be included and succeed.
- **Personalize your approach.** Understand that belonging is different for everybody.

While activities like these help, let's not guess on belonging. Think of the *precision medicine* approach to care, where we provide a treatment plan based on the individual. Marcia Horn, president and CEO of the International Cancer Advocacy Network, a not-for-profit organization that assists people with cancer, lets each person know that they are an individual. No two people are alike. She calls the approach $N = 1$ to signify that in statistical terms, everyone is an N *of 1*. We can adapt this mindset by creating conditions that make each person feel they belong. There will be consistency in many areas; however, by asking each person what is important to them, we help create the feeling that "this is the place for me."

A SURPRISING WAY TO MAKE A CONNECTION: ASK SOMEBODY FOR A FAVOR

An important part of belonging is being asked to help. People in healthcare are natural problem solvers. There is magic in the question "What do you think?" It shows respect, demonstrates listening, and lets people know that you trust them. A big win is that this question provides an opportunity for open and honest feedback and conversation. This is a hard one for some leaders because of their empathy for their team. They think, "How can I ask them to do one more thing when they are so busy?" However, engaged people want the organization to do well. They become more engaged by being asked for their thoughts.

Years ago, a facilitator shared what she does if someone at an event asks a question she's not sure how to answer. After all, she is seen as the expert. She said that she asks the group what *they* think. The answer that comes back is better than hers would have been. Take every opportunity to ask, "What do you think we should do?"

Communication is addressed throughout this book. In a recent study that Healthcare Plus Solutions Group, LLC, funded about models of care, themes emerged around communication, which connects to belonging.[9] We found a critical gap between how leaders view solutions and how frontline workers view them. The big reason for the gap is that the front line are not brought into the conversation soon enough.

People want to have input into decisions that affect their work. When we give them a chance to weigh in, they feel a sense of ownership, which supports belonging. When Houston Methodist designed a new outpatient center building, they prioritized employee belonging and patient experience. They invited employees to help name the patient rooms. The majority of the artwork on the walls was created by employees. Houston Methodist even reserved the 23rd floor, with the best view in the organization, for an employee gym to send the message, "This is your building. You belong here, and we saved the best for you."

FOSTERING GOOD COWORKER RELATIONSHIPS

The importance of coworker relationships cannot be overstated. We know that having friends at work makes a big difference in how people feel about their job. The 2023 Society for Human Resource Management (SHRM) Workplace Romance and Relationships Survey found that US employees who have close friends at work are much more likely to say they feel a strong sense of belonging than those who don't.[10] The survey also suggested that having close friends at work improves retention. Here are some strategies leaders can use to help foster relationships and belonging on their teams.

Create a culture of accountability. While it's not possible to force friendships, leaders can do a lot to encourage strong, positive coworker relationships. One tactic is to create a culture of accountability. When people are held accountable for meeting deadlines, completing assignments, and fulfilling their obligations to the team, there will be less dissension and more harmony between coworkers. People won't resent coworkers for "coasting" or requiring others to pick up their slack. This culture also includes accountability for hurtful behaviors. People will struggle to belong if gossip, aggression, belittling, or other unprofessional behaviors of other team members are tolerated by the leader.

Establish group norms and make them explicit. Take steps to ensure that people treat others with fairness and respect. A Standards of Behavior document that explains what's acceptable and unacceptable is a powerful tool. The idea is to spell out what "right" looks like—avoid gossip, knock on doors rather than barging in, smile and say good morning, etc.—and have people sign the document. This keeps people aware of their behavior and paves the way for positive interactions between coworkers.

Celebrate together. Finally, the more that employees spend time together and get to know each other as people (not just workers), the closer they will become. The idea is to create a sense of community. This can include team-building activities, social events, or volunteer opportunities. Look for ways to bring people together. A great way to do this is to celebrate employees' personal milestones, such as a marriage, a new home, or a new baby. Birthdays matter too. All of these celebrations strengthen coworker bonds and make friendships more likely to develop. Be mindful that activities outside of working hours may be perceived differently by employees with heavy family or caregiving obligations.

Foster psychological safety. It is important to make sure there is a high degree of psychological safety in the workplace. This is a critical factor in helping employees feel that they belong. When people know they can tell the truth without negative reactions from leaders and team members, they won't bottle things up and distance themselves. When ideas are shared, be sure to give them a chance to be explored rather than shutting down the discussion. Employees will feel free to express themselves, voice their opinions, and take the kinds of risks we want them to take—the kinds that lead to collaboration, innovation, and meaningful work. All of this is needed for employees to flourish.

Belonging is vital for retention, but the benefits are so much more than that. When a person feels that they belong in their workplace, their willingness to offer ideas on how to improve operations is elevated. They are more likely to share their thoughts in an open and honest fashion. They will take more risks (in a good way) because they feel they are in this for the long haul. They represent the organization in a positive way, both inside and outside the workplace. Bottom line: belonging is good for our people and good for business.

By prioritizing belonging, we can help each person feel, "This is the place for me. I would not want to be anywhere else."

REFERENCES

1. McKinsey & Company. 2020. "Diversity Wins: How Inclusion Matters." Published May 19. http://mckinsey.com/featured-insights/diversity-and-inclusion/diversity-wins-how-inclusion-matters.

2. Lean In. 2022. "Women in the Workplace: Key Findings 2022." McKinsey & Company. http://leanin.org/women-in-the-workplace/2022.

3. De Smet, A., B. Dowling, B. Hancock, and B. Schaninger. 2022. "The Great Attrition Is Making Hiring Harder. Are You Searching the Right Talent Pools?" *McKinsey Quarterly*. Published July. http://mckinsey.com/~/media/mckinsey/business%20functions/people%20and%20organizational%20performance/our%20insights/the%20great%20attrition%20is%20making%20hiring%20harder%20are%20you%20searching%20the%20right%20talent%20pools/the-great-attrition-is-making-hiring-harder-vf.pdf.

4. Cigna. 2020. "Loneliness and the Impact." Published January. https://cigna.com/static/www-cigna-com/docs/health-care-providers/resources/loneliness-index-provider-flyer.pdf.

5. Holt-Lunstad, J., T. B. Smith, M. Baker, T. Harris, and D. Stephenson. 2015. "Loneliness and Social Isolation as Risk Factors for Mortality: A Meta-analytic Review." *Perspectives on Psychological Science* 10(2): 227–37.

6. Allen, K.-A., M. L. Kern, C. S. Rozek, D. McInereney, and G. M. Slavich. 2021. "Belonging: A Review of Conceptual Issues, an Integrative Framework, and Directions for Future Research." *Australian Journal of Psychology* 73(1): 87–102.

7. Dansereau Jr., F., G. Graen, and W. J. Haga. 1975. "A Vertical Dyad Linkage Approach to Leadership Within Formal Organizations: A Longitudinal Investigation of the Role Making Process." *Organizational Behavior and Human Performance* 13(1): 46–78.

8. Tajfel, H., and J. Turner. 1979. "An Integrative Theory of Intergroup Conflict." In M. J. Hatch and M. Schultz (eds.), *Organizational Identity: A Reader*. Oxford: Oxford University Press.

9. Joslin Insight. 2023. *Models of Care: Insight Study*. Published March 23. http://healthcareplussg.com/models-of-care -insight-study-results.

10. Navarra, K. 2023. "Workplace Romances Can Be Tricky, but Friendships Boost Retention." SHRM Research Institute. Published February 7. https://www.shrm.org/resourcesandtools /hr-topics/employee-relations/pages/workplace-romances -can-be-tricky-but-friendships-boost-retention.aspx.

CHAPTER 6

Recognition and Appreciation

RECOGNITION IS A critical element of building trust. When our positive contributions are noticed and appreciated, we are more likely to trust that we will continue to be valued and appreciated in the future. We begin to trust in our leaders when we feel that they see the energy, passion, and effort we put into our work and that they appreciate us for who we are.

Employee recognition has always mattered, but now it matters more than ever. Our industry faces continuous disruptions and a widespread talent shortage. People are stressed, anxious, and burned out. It has never been so important for leaders to create organizations where people want to be—workplaces that replenish them, fill their cups, and set them up to flourish.

Regular recognition is a powerful force. It keeps people coming to work when times are tough. It builds up the emotional bank account that keeps people engaged and connected to passion and purpose. It fosters belonging and engagement. It strengthens relationships and builds camaraderie. All of these things improve retention.

WHY DOES RECOGNITION MATTER?

Recognition continued to show up in our analysis as a major element of well-being and of intention to stay within the organization and recommend it to others.[1] Satisfaction with recognition was even protective against symptoms of post-traumatic stress.[2] In other large studies, failure to recognize employee performance was 2.9 times more likely than compensation to result in turnover.[3] In our research, less than 50 percent of healthcare workers were satisfied with their recognition at work. The great news for financially strained organizations is that recognition is often free.

Beyond satisfying the human desire for recognition, showing appreciation to others is a form of expressing gratitude. Numerous individual health benefits are associated with expressing gratitude, including improved happiness, decreased anxiety and depression, and improved cardiovascular health.[4] Appreciation of others is a win-win for both the giver and the receiver of the praise.

It is also important to note that some mark a distinction between recognition and appreciation and argue that employees need both.[5] Recognition is based on a job well done or a specific achievement. Appreciation is about acknowledging that the employee is important and valuable just because of who they *are*.

RECOGNITION MOVES RESULTS

We've already said recognition is a replenisher, relationship-builder, and transformer of cultures. But how does it do these things? Here are just a few ways that a culture of recognition pays off:

- **Focusing on recognition shifts our mindset.** Healthcare leaders are conditioned to look for what's wrong and to fix it. When we get in the habit of seeking out people to recognize, we shift our mindset to what's working well rather than what's not. Coming from a place of positivity and gratitude changes everything. It engages others and invigorates you.
- **It makes it easier to move and sustain results.** What gets recognized gets repeated, and this helps build consistency.

When we recognize someone, we have the opportunity to create success templates. Immediately identify what went well—and more importantly, why it went well—to achieve the better results. Document those items so that they can be repeated to achieve more progress in the future. If outcomes go backwards, get back on track by checking to see whether some of the successful actions had been reduced.

- **It's a powerful coaching and education tool.** When we recognize someone for doing something right, we impact more than the person being recognized. Others around them will notice and emulate the recognized behavior. This gives others a chance to learn and adopt best practices. The behavior can be shared broadly through coaching so that the whole organization can learn how to practice it.
- **It makes things feel more doable.** When people get recognized for doing hard things, it makes success at the task feel possible to the rest of the organization. The person who is recognized is usually more than willing to coach others on the same journey.

WHAT KEEPS US FROM PRACTICING RECOGNITION AND APPRECIATION?

Leaders want to do the right thing. We want people to feel good—about themselves, about us, and about the organization. So why don't we make recognition and appreciation a priority? There can be many reasons.

It might be that we overcomplicate recognition. We assume we don't have time to do it well. We may not realize that the best forms of recognition aren't complex or forced. They're an organic part of how we manage the organization. They're just part of the job.

Maybe we think conditions have to be perfect, or maybe we are waiting for the right time. We might feel overwhelmed or busy, and recognition doesn't feel as urgent as other tasks. The truth is that we don't need a big milestone or huge achievement to recognize someone.

Sometimes we just aren't clear on what to recognize people *for*. What matters most to them? Consider asking people what aspects of their work they're the most excited about—knowledge of what's meaningful to them often points us in the direction of their biggest achievements.

Employees themselves can discourage us. It is not unusual to hear someone say, "I don't need recognition." Of course they do! Whether we know it or not, we all flourish when our hard work is recognized and when we feel appreciated for our unique strengths, abilities, and personalities.

Leaders, too, may have their own biases against providing recognition. For example:

- "I don't need it, so why do they?"
- "That is their job. It's what they are being paid to do."
- "They will get a big head if they are complimented too much."
- "Weren't they recognized not that long ago?" (As if there is a quota that limits recognition!)
- "Others will be upset if someone gets recognized and they don't."
- "We only recognize those who go above and beyond."

None of these are good reasons not to provide recognition and reap the many rewards that come along with it.

HOW DO PEOPLE WANT TO BE RECOGNIZED OR APPRECIATED?

We asked people how they wanted to be recognized or appreciated. To be honest, a lot of people said more money. But is it really about the money?

Money is an expression of value. It is an objective, external symbol of worth. When people described wanting more money, they often said things such as "Pay me what *I'm worth*." The request for more money as a sign of appreciation is a request to have one's worth and contribution to the organization validated; it is not only about a few extra dollars in the bank account.

Because money is objective and measurable, we feel devalued when we perceive that others are getting more than we are for working the same amount or less. Inequities in pay not only result in some employees receiving fewer dollars; they also give employees the feeling that the organization is saying they are worth *less* than others. It makes them feel unappreciated, regardless of the actual dollar amount.

Many healthcare organizations are under financial strain, which isn't going away anytime soon. This is where some people get discouraged. If employees want money and we don't have it, are we out of options? Don't fret—luckily, people also wanted a lot of things that are free.

Here are some examples from our research of things people said when we asked how they would like to be recognized or appreciated:

- "More frequent rounds by leadership to see our struggle."
- "A better understanding of our daily workflow by members of leadership would be helpful . . . them shadowing frontline staff and spending time with us [so] they can more personally be in tune with needs."
- "Just a simple thank-you every now and then would suffice."
- "Just a simple 'good morning' or 'thank-you' would be greatly appreciated."[6]

Many of these actions require an investment of time and intentionality but not money. It is interesting that in these comments people are asking for things that could come not only from their direct supervisors and teammates but also from their leaders. This tells us that recognition and appreciation efforts need to be happening at all levels—this isn't something that can be fully delegated.

Many organizations have awards that are given monthly or annually, such as employee of the month or year. That is good, but it affects only a few people. A good recognition strategy makes it easy for people to recognize and appreciate one another frequently at all levels of the organization.

An undervalued source of appreciation for employees doesn't come from management or leadership; it comes from each other. Yes, people want to hear praise from their supervisors and leaders. However, a sincere compliment from an admired coworker goes a long way and helps foster a sense of belonging. Regardless of what programs are in place for recognition, you can start with recognizing your fellow humans right now.

A surgeon was sharing how he recognizes the operating room staff. As a surgeon, he gets a lot of appreciation for the life-improving pediatric surgeries he performs. But after each case, he also makes sure to shake the hand of everyone in the room—scrub techs, nurses, and anesthesiologists—saying, "Thank you, we did it! Great case!" *We.* By taking 30 seconds to appreciate the contributions of the whole team, he is making recognition a regular part of his daily workflow.

In healthcare, people work so hard. They do many things that deserve recognition, so many that at times they may feel they are being taken for granted. Letting people know that we appreciate them, care about them, and are thinking about them is invaluable. We know such actions make a difference, but sometimes we underestimate just how much of a difference they make.

HOW TO RECOGNIZE OTHERS: A FEW BEST PRACTICES

It's easy to recognize big achievements and milestones like birthdays and length of service. These are important, but it's often more meaningful to catch people doing good things in the moment. There are endless opportunities to recognize people: during rounding, in meetings, in huddles. For example, you can start every huddle by telling a story that highlights the difference the team makes. You can start every meeting by asking each person to recognize someone else.

Here are a few best practices for creating a rich and sustainable culture of recognition.

- **Consistency matters.** Make appreciation a part of your daily routine. Don't wait until it's convenient or when you feel you have time. It will never get done. Put it on your calendar so that it becomes a habit. You might choose to spend the last 15 minutes of each day recognizing people.
- **Become a world-class noticer.** Talk to employees often. Pay attention when rounding. Whom do patients consistently mention? Whose rooms are the cleanest? Who jumps in to help with a cheerful attitude and smile? The idea is to notice the everyday things people do.
- **Recognize the person as soon as possible after their action.** The longer you wait, the less effective your recognition will be. This makes recognition more organic, natural, and sincere.
- **Ask people how they want to be recognized.** Some thrive on public recognition while others would prefer a quiet thank-you or a handwritten note. Everyone is different. Measure how people feel about the recognition they receive, and identify which departments or units can be recognized more effectively.
- **Don't wait for huge milestones. It's okay to appreciate people for doing their job.** When Cal Ripken Jr. broke Lou Gehrig's major-league record for playing consecutive games, TV stations interrupted regular programming to celebrate the accomplishment. They stopped the game so Cal could run around the perimeter of the field to be recognized—all for playing 162 games a year and being paid very well to do so. If Cal could be recognized for doing what he was paid to do, why can't people who work in healthcare?[7]

- **Don't wait for perfection.** Recognize people where they are (then raise the bar). When Quint worked at Holy Cross in Chicago, there was a hospital-wide celebration when they hit the 40th percentile in patient satisfaction. They celebrated the progress. Then they raised the bar and said, "Now let's get to the 60th percentile, then the 75th, then the 90th, then the 99th." Eventually they ended up in the top percentile in patient experience. If they had waited until they reached the end goal, they would have had a long wait indeed!

- **Connect to the organization's mission, values, or standards of behavior.** You might tell someone, "John, I saw that you walked that person to the imaging department instead of pointing. I know that helped the person and demonstrates our value of teamwork" or "Katrina, when you went home yesterday, the work area was left in great shape. Thank you. That makes such a difference and demonstrates a commitment to our coworker standards."

- **Peer-to-peer shout-outs can be extremely valuable.** Peers are close to the action and see the ordinary things that people do well. Encourage this and make it easy.

  For example, in a hospital's food service department, the director was getting great results. Near the entrance to the department, there was a sign with bold letters that said, "MAD. You can do it." Each day, each person is encouraged to notice others who are making a difference (MAD). The department has simple forms for writing down the names of such people and what they do. The recognized person could be a coworker in food service, a coworker in the hospital, a physician, someone in leadership, or a volunteer. These small forms are then placed in a large, clear container. Each week some forms are selected, read, and put on display. Leaders read all the forms. Everyone who is listed is made aware that they have been named and by whom.

It is fun and it works. One can hear people encouraging each other to "get MAD today." Best of all, this department has superb results across the board.

- **Make writing thank-you notes part of your routine.** They are an incredible form of recognition. People truly cherish them.

One hospital recognized its employee of the month by placing a box in the cafeteria with a story about why that person had been selected. Beside the box was a stack of index cards and an invitation for staff to write something nice about the person. Maybe it was a thank-you, a story they wanted to share, or just a note saying congratulations. At the end of the month, the employee would be given the index cards along with a commemorative pin to wear.

A manager in that hospital attended the wake of an employee who had passed away. As she approached the casket, she noticed his employee-of-the-month pin attached to his lapel. Placed in the casket were the many index cards he had received. The man's wife shared with the manager that as he was dying, he kept those cards by his bedside and often read them. Never underestimate the power of such gestures.

Make thank-you notes a regular part of your leaders' schedules. Ideally, the notes are handwritten and sent to the person's home. Typed notes can work when they are specific and personalized.

It is not unusual for leaders to think they are sending more notes than they are. Put reminders on your calendar to block out time for writing notes. Check when they have been sent. Writing just 10 notes a week for 48 weeks of the year would end up being 480 notes. That's a lot of notes! However, in an organization of 1,800 employees, that means each employee would receive one note over a four-year period. Do the math.

- **Be careful with group recognition.** There are times when a leader will recognize everyone. Whenever possible, it is good to say, "Thank you. You all are doing a great job." Just make sure this statement is accurate. If there is a low performer in the department, the staff know it. When a group thank-you includes this person, the staff starts to feel that the leader is not on top of things. Sometimes leaders ask, "Won't people feel bad when others are recognized and they are not?" The key is to make sure the recognition is for specific results.

  A hospital with seven inpatient units had two units that did well in patient experience. The hospital's CEO was encouraged to recognize these two units and their leaders in the department meeting and to connect their performance to the outcomes (e.g., "This outcome means that patients in those areas feel more listened to or better understand discharge plans"). He was concerned that he would be hurting the other five unit leaders. But he wasn't. He was recognizing important outcomes and those leaders who were achieving them.

  Though hesitant, he did it. The next month, there were three of seven units to recognize. By the fifth month, all seven were recognized. As mentioned earlier, recognized behavior gets repeated and emulated. This technique also helps others know whom they can learn from.
- **Finally, recognize the recognizers.** You definitely want this behavior repeated!

CEREMONIES AND CELEBRATIONS

Ceremonies have a tremendous effect. Think about the power of pinning ceremonies for nurses. Each nurse receives a pin that is put on them by a person of their choice. Often this is followed by each nurse lighting a candle that they take home. White-coat ceremonies for medical students are similar. Families are there. It is as important as the ceremony when a person in flight school or in the service receives their wings or other insignia.

People in healthcare seem to like recognition that they can wear. At Baptist Hospital in Pensacola, Florida, employees who made a suggestion that was acted on received a pin in the shape of a light bulb, signifying a bright idea. *USA Today* did a story on the hospital. The light bulbs caught the attention of the reporter. As she talked with staff, she would ask them about the light-bulb pins. Each person was proud to explain what had earned them the pin, known as a Bright Ideas pin.

Aramark Healthcare+ has created what it calls the Presidential Eleos Recognition program. Named after Eleos, the Greek goddess of compassion, the program is designed to acknowledge those who go above and beyond in embodying the organization's brand values of compassion, empathy, and excellence. At any time, the CEO can present a special teammate or employee with a unique coin to recognize their exceptional contributions to the company and the patients, caregivers, and clients it serves. These coins are highly prized and have truly inspired employees to live the Aramark mission.

Celebrations of all sorts are extremely meaningful and powerful. One hospital president shared that she holds some sort of celebration during each quarter, even if it's just handing out treats for all shifts. When asked what she did when there were no outcomes to celebrate, she gave a smirk and said, "We find something." She was right. Even in the toughest times, there are things to recognize and celebrate.

It is tempting to scale back on recognition and ceremony, especially when times are tough financially. One organization was considering canceling the annual staff recognition event as a cost-saving measure. This event celebrated lengths of service in five-year increments. Fortunately, they paused and asked past attendees. They heard from the staff that this event was a big deal to honorees. Many purchased special clothes to wear to it. They were able to have some family members present. They had professional photos taken. They received mementos. It was *their* night. For some, it was one of the highlights of their career. Often the department would then have a celebration for members who received recognition. If an employee worked for the organization for 30 years and attended the celebration every five years, that meant six special nights for them. The investment sure seemed worth it. The senior executives changed their mind, and the recognition events continued.

RECOGNITION AND INNOVATION GO HAND IN HAND: BRIGHT IDEAS PROGRAMS

Innovation is a key word in healthcare, and there is lots of it. Remember that story you just read about the *USA Today* reporter asking the people about their "Bright Ideas" pins? "Bright Ideas" programs give all employees a chance to submit ideas for the organization (not just in their area—ideas can be submitted for anything). These programs create plenty of opportunities for people to be recognized. Often they result in great ideas that end up improving service, improving quality, saving the organization money, or all of the above.

Provide leaders with ways to evaluate the ideas collected. It is like mining for gold. There will be lots of misses before the gold nuggets appear. The key is to acknowledge the employee's creativity and contribution even if the idea can't be implemented as proposed. To keep the good ideas coming, take time to discuss where the employee is coming from. Can the idea be adapted in some manner? Can some of it be tried for a while to see if it works? If the idea is adopted, publicize who originated it.

Quantity is good. Be sure you are encouraging as many people as possible to share their ideas. Keep submission forms simple! Just ask for a summary of the idea and how it will help.

Put all ideas in a container, and each month draw some out and recognize the employees who submitted them even if the ideas were not implemented, as this encourages engagement. In fact, you might give out awards for submissions. Have implemented ideas in another container. Draw those out as well, even though some people will receive additional thanks. You can even weight the ideas according to impact.

Make ideas part of a person's annual review. Just note whether they have submitted an idea. It is okay if coworkers helped them. It builds team collaboration.

Early on, some leaders may see this as more work, and it is. The leaders' skills in soliciting, recognizing, and implementing ideas will need development. A good starting approach to is to pick a topic and ask for ideas. For example: "Our patient no-show rates are climbing. We don't want people to not receive the care they need. What are some suggestions to address this?"

Get in the habit of looking closely at ideas to find the value. Can some parts of an idea be implemented? Can some ideas be piloted at first to see how they do? Can you form a group to review rejected ideas just to see whether there are second opinions? If someone does not review rejected ideas, it is possible that good ones will be missed.

By collecting bright ideas, you also get insight into how frontline folks see the organization. The late Dr. Floyd (Fred) Loop was CEO of the Cleveland Clinic at a time when it was struggling. Dr. Loop laid the foundation for what the organization is today. He introduced world-class care, and he loved ideas. As CEO, he personally read every idea that came in. Why? Because it helped him learn so much about what was happening. He spotted talent in those who turned ideas in. He noticed who turned down ideas. Early on, people may say no too quickly: "We don't have money for that." Dr. Loop would see the value and help find the money.

DON'T OVERLOOK PHYSICIANS, LEADERS, AND PARTNERS

Of course it's important to recognize clinicians, caregivers, and the frontline service workers who prepare patient meals, keep their rooms sparkling clean, and transport them to surgery. We also need to think about the vendors and outside partners who help make our organizations work. And don't overlook leaders and physicians, two groups that can at times get taken for granted. We sometimes think they don't seem to need as much recognition.

The response a healthcare system in Boston got when they celebrated National Doctor's Day shows just how much physicians appreciate recognition. Here's what happened. Leaders asked staff members to write letters expressing what physicians meant to them. The stories that came back were amazing! The leaders posted these letters outside the cafeteria, and for a week that hallway was filled with physicians and visitors reading these strong, positive, powerful stories.

The letters had an incredible effect on the doctors. The results were so inspiring that for Nurses' Week, the organization asked the doctors to turn the tables. Nearly 100 percent of the physicians came through with their own letters about nurses. It was interesting to note that many doctors were better at sharing what nurses meant to them in writing than verbally. (One doctor even wrote a beautiful, heartfelt poem.) It was wonderful to see the floodgate of positive emotions, appreciation, and gratitude that this health system unleashed just by asking people to share their thoughts and feelings on the people who work with them.

Our leaders need appreciation, too. These jobs are harder than they look. Sometimes it is like being the sound and light technician at a concert—nobody notices when it goes well, but everyone can see when it doesn't. Take a moment to send your leader a note when they have done something you appreciate. If they are having to make tough decisions, be empathic. If they make a mistake, forgive them and remember that they get a lot of things right. Although they may act like they don't need it, a little recognition goes a long way.

DON'T UNDERESTIMATE YOUR IMPACT

Everyone is important and makes a difference in the lives of those around them. When people who are in a leadership role recognize this truth about someone, it has a bigger impact. It is a deeply meaningful form of recognition.

Remember Dr. Loop from the Cleveland Clinic? One day he shared that he was in the public restroom and that it was very clean. As he was washing his hands, an Environmental Services (EVS) worker came in to check the restroom. Dr. Loop introduced himself, then complimented him and the EVS team on the cleanliness of the restroom and the difference it made. Dr. Loop said the person's smile lit up the room. He was surprised about the effect his comment had.

Don't underestimate your impact in helping people recognize *their* impact. There is no small recognition.

Recognition works. It's that simple. The beauty of creating a culture of recognition is that it makes life better for everyone, including ourselves. Recognition fills your cup. The more we uplift people, remind them of their purpose, and connect them back to their calling, the more we do the same for ourselves. Together, we improve the human margin and help one another flourish.

REFERENCES

1. Meese, K. A., L. Boitet, A. Gorman, N. Patel, L. Nassetta, and D. A. Rogers. 2023. "Don't Go: Examining the Relationships Between Purpose, Work Environment and Turnover Intention Across the Entire Healthcare Team." Dublin: European Academy of Management annual meeting.

2. Boitet, L. M., K. A. Meese, M. Hays, C. A. Gorman, K. L. Swee-ney, and D. A. Rogers. 2023. "Burnout, Moral Distress, and Compassion Fatigue as Correlates of Post-Traumatic Stress Symptoms in Clinical and Non-Clinical Healthcare Workers." *Journal of Healthcare Management* (forthcoming).

3. Sull, D., C. Sull, and B. Zweig. 2022. "Toxic Culture Is Driv-ing the Great Resignation." *MIT Sloan Management Review* 63(2): 1–9.

4. Emmons, R. A. 2007. *Thanks!: How the New Science of Gratitude Can Make You Happier.* Boston: Houghton Mifflin Harcourt.

5. Robbins, M. 2019. "Why Employees Need Both Recogni-tion and Appreciation." *Harvard Business Review.* Published November 12. http://hbr.org/2019/11/why-employees-need -both-recognition-and-appreciation.

6. Meese, K. A. Unpublished data. (Details of this work are provided in the Appendix.)

7. Baseball Reference. 2009. "Cal Ripkin Jr." Accessed Sep-tember 7, 2023. http://baseball-reference.com/players /r/ripkeca01.shtml.

CHAPTER 7

Communication

COMMUNICATION HAS ALWAYS been important, especially in a high-stakes industry like healthcare. In times of rapid change and uncertainty, it becomes even more important.

Communication is one of the best tools we have for building trust. It helps us build relationships, demonstrate alignment with our values, and show care and concern for our people. It helps us make sure that employees understand the reasons behind decisions, and it clears up misunderstandings that erode trust. A leader's ability to provide consistent, values-aligned, real-time communication is fuel for everything else. Furthermore, good communication is the most powerful tool we have in closing the gap between what leaders are actually doing and what people think they are doing.

Only 7 percent of US workers strongly agree that they get timely, accurate, and open communication at work. This is concerning because research has shown that good communication results in greater engagement and intention to stay within the organization.[1]

Good communication is not a nice-to-have. It's an essential leadership skill. Without it, much of our hard work and great ideas may never come to fruition. Yet while we may know how important communication is, focusing on it is not easy when a leader is dealing with a multitude of demands. In employee engagement surveys, *communication* is often identified as one of the top items that could be improved. This is true even when communication is quite good.

HOW GOOD COMMUNICATION HELPS YOUR ORGANIZATION THRIVE

The good news is that when we're able to identify and fix communication issues, we may see positive changes right away. Here are just a few of the benefits of great communication:

- It creates clarity. People know what is expected. Clarity enhances performance, helps teams meet their goals, and prevents mistakes and misunderstanding. Communication about expectations of employees was ranked as the most important form of communication in Gallup's research. Employees are 2.8 times more likely to be engaged when they speak with their manager regularly about their goals and progress.[1]
- It fills emotional bank accounts. It demonstrates empathy and understanding and shows that we care. When we handle communication the right way—even when we're asking people to make incredibly tough changes—we can strengthen relationships and positively affect the entire organization. It keeps people engaged and connected—to one another and to their sense of purpose.
- It reduces anxiety. No one likes vagueness and fuzzy boundaries. When we communicate in ways that make it clear what needs to happen next, what right looks like, and how performance will be measured, we remove the uncertainty that keeps people fretting and second-guessing and prevents them from doing their best work.
- Along with skill development, it pushes responsibility and authority to the front lines. This is important in healthcare, where we have to act quickly and decisively.
- It closes the trust gap. As mentioned earlier, research shows a gap between what leaders are actually doing

and what people think they are doing, which can lead to distrust. Good communication can heal this divide.

- It stops misinformation. Communication shortfalls lead to a lot of speculation and gossip around what's really going on. Misinformation spreads. When there is an information void, people fill it with worst-case-scenario thinking.
- It is at the core of emotionally intelligent leadership. It better connects the leader with their team. It creates psychological safety, which in turn creates a culture where people feel comfortable giving honest feedback and sharing their ideas and opinions.
- It keeps organizations aligned, nimble, adaptive, and able to innovate. Great communication is the oil that keeps the machine running smoothly.

Ultimately, the right kind of communication creates a place where people want to be.

WHAT KEEPS LEADERS FROM COMMUNICATING WELL?

Many factors can make clear and timely communication difficult:

- People have "full plates." Busy schedules and competing priorities can cause communication to fall by the wayside.
- There is too much uncertainty and complexity. When things are rapidly changing and we're constantly bombarded with new information, it's a struggle to provide clear and accurate information to employees.
- We may tend to want to wait for things to be perfect before we share information. (When we don't know the final answer, we can say, "Here's what we know now; you will be updated as we learn more.")

- The need for repetition and the use of multiple channels can be underestimated. (Better to overcommunicate than undercommunicate. If something is important, you need to say it "in 100 ways for 100 days.")
- With so many demands on your time, being a patient listener can be hard.
- We don't know how to answer tough questions, so we avoid people until we have an answer. (See chapter 4 for an exercise on how to respond to tough questions.)
- We forget that our own knowledge and background provide understanding of an issue, and we wrongly assume that others already have the understanding or context to interpret the information.

It's important to be on the lookout for red flags in communication. Sure, our employee engagement surveys may tell us there's an issue, but we may also see signs in real time. For example, people may have trouble executing tasks, and things don't get done. Tasks may seem harder than they ought to be. Employees may seem unhappy. In general, there's a sense of uneasiness.

PLAYING OFFENSE ON COMMUNICATION

Ask people what good communication looks like *to them*. As leaders, we might assume that we know the best way to communicate with our teams in a way that gets heard. However, that may not always be true. Asking people how they want to receive communication is a game changer.

Here's how it works. Each leader meets with their direct reports and says, "Good communication is important to us. We know that a lot of people have different preferences. I want to hear what good communication looks like to you." Then go around the room and ask each person to weigh in. The idea is to get everyone on the same page.

You might need to keep asking for clarification. If they say, "We just want to know what's going on," you might respond, "Let's talk about a time that we had really good communication. What did that look like?" Also ask them to be specific about a time when something wasn't communicated well or in a timely fashion. Really drill down. Finally, say, "Tell me what information you would like."

Ask People: How Do You Want to Get Your Information?

After everyone has had an opportunity to speak, say, "Now here's some information we, as an organization, want you to have." Then share the goals you want people to meet. Explain why they are important.

Next, ask the group, "How do you want to receive this communication? Do you want to receive an email? Should we post it somewhere? Is a video helpful?" The idea is to let the department decide how information is going to be provided (see feature box).

Communication Methods

There are lots of different avenues for communication to choose from.

Leadership team meetings and monthly senior leader meetings. Many health systems hold routine leadership meetings, bringing administrative and clinical leaders together for information sharing or training. This is a great time to communicate key messages. At these meetings, provide talking points that will be cascaded to supervisors and frontline team members.

Town hall meetings. These are especially good for helping big systems push out urgent messages. The CEO and other members of the senior leadership team might go on the road and conduct these forums every quarter. They can be in-person, virtual, or ideally both. (During COVID, many organizations held town halls weekly.) Include all team members and make sure people can ask questions.

Emails, newsletters, and other written messages. These can be quick and easy to create. Just don't overwhelm people with too much content. Be aware that many clinicians and frontline employees are not sitting in front of a computer checking emails all day. Email may not be the most effective mode of communication for these employees.

Video updates. Employees prefer to receive certain messages—such as information on a big change or a crisis event—directly from the top. A video update is the next-best thing besides a face-to-face meeting. At times video can feel more authentic than a written message. It can also humanize the person delivering the message. Make sure to consider whether the issue needs feedback and interaction or whether it is appropriate for one-way communication.

Weekly rounding. The idea is that leaders take time to touch base with employees, make a personal connection, and find out what is (and isn't) working well. Leader rounding on staff is the single best way to raise employee satisfaction and loyalty and to attract and retain high performers. It allows for rich two-way communication and an option to clarify misunderstandings in real time before they spread.

Daily huddles. These can occur throughout the health system in every unit, department, and division. Not only are huddles a good way for leaders to share timely messages and updates, but they are also great for bidirectional communication. They allow information to cascade upward: from front line to hospital to division to senior leadership. An added bonus is that daily huddles, when used to check in with each other, can also improve well-being and engagement.[2]

Some important messages may require all of these methods. It's better to err on the side of saying something too many times versus not saying it enough.

Narrate Their Responsibility in the Process

After all the topics above have been discussed and everyone has shared their preferences, it's time to say, "Now that we have agreed on how you want to receive these vital communications, how can we make sure people access them? And what are your suggestions on how to address people who do not read or view them?" Since they have had so much input into creating the process, there ought to be no reason for them to object. These questions, along with the answers they elicit, really create accountability.

There are several wins with this approach. One, everyone gains clarity on what excellent communication looks like. Two, staff commit to being accountable for reading email messages, watching videos, and so forth. Three, managers enjoy a sense of relief because now they are not trying to hit a vague target.

"GREAT MEETING! WHAT'S NEXT?": GETTING INTENTIONAL WITH MESSAGING AND ACTIONS

One issue that some leaders can struggle with at times is translating what happens in meetings into action. Most of us have had this experience. We have a great meeting that produces lots of great ideas. Then the meeting ends, we go back to work, and all energy that was generated just stalls. What we decided in the meeting—or what we think we decided—doesn't get to the right people.

The key is to get intentional about moving information out of the meeting and sharing it with the right people in the right way. Here is a framework that can help:

1. How do we keep this messaging connected to our core values and mission?
2. What groups need to receive the communication? System wide? Certain entities? Specific departments?
3. What are the main message points? It is so important to include the "why" behind decisions.
4. What actions, if any, are the receivers of the communication expected to take? Be really clear and specific here.
5. If there is a burning platform, what is it? (The burning platform is the piece that captures the heart and mind of the recipient and compels them to act.)
6. How is the message to be delivered: print, video, or in person?

CREATING THE BEST ODDS FOR BEING HEARD

Even if you think you've communicated something—even if you have said it more than once and via more than one method—your responsibility doesn't stop there. It's also on you to make sure that listeners understand what you're saying.

While you probably can't be certain your message was received 100 percent of the time, there are things you can do to improve the odds:

- **Make messages simple and clear.** Don't overcomplicate things. Sometimes leaders do this because they're insecure, but it's more likely because they don't take the time to organize their thoughts. Use simple words and short sentences. Think carefully about the message structure. Figure out the main takeaway you want to convey and work backward from there—don't lead with the details.

- **Keep messaging consistent.** A big challenge of communicating with groups is that not everyone hears what we say the same way. Often, we say so much that people may not recognize which points are the most important. This is why, when we share information that's meant to be cascaded, we standardize the talking points. Consistency is everything. To make sure everyone gets the message, we need to be sure we clarify it and disseminate it across the organization the right way.

- **Let people teach-back the key points.** The teach-back method is where we check for understanding by asking people to explain it back to us.[3] We need to make sure the key message points are not missed. If you ask after a meeting what the top three takeaways are, you are likely to get as many different answers as there are people in the room. Take a pause after each agenda item has been discussed (you can even say, "Pause"). Invite people to ask clarifying questions, at which point you can decide whether those questions need to be addressed outside this meeting. If the answer is no, just go right to the next agenda item. If it is yes, then you can ask, "Okay, so what are the bullet points we're going to roll out? Who's going to do that? When and how are they going to be rolled out?"

- **Cascade information for smart sequencing.** Because healthcare organizations are built on shift work, not everyone can hear every message at the same time. Someone is going to hear it last. That's one part of the problem. Another part is that this person may hear it from another employee, not a leader. This immediately creates distrust. They feel like they are always the last to know. In addition, it's possible that the other employee didn't effectively communicate the information, which leads to misinformation and gossip. Rather than waiting for information to trickle down from the top through various levels of leadership, it is better if senior leaders at the initial meeting agrees to cascade the information they learned to their teams at the same time. That way, instead of having eight different cascades, one big cascade happens simultaneously throughout the organization.

- **Watch the timing of your messages. Be sensitive to how employees might be feeling.** Consider the tone of the message against the backdrop of other things going on in the organization. Celebratory messages that come when employees are feeling overwhelmed, burned out, and exhausted can have the potential to damage trust or create a perception that leaders don't care.

- **Beware the untold story.** Because we are sensemaking beings who seek to understand, in the absence of a story people will make up their own. People tend to connect dots between different organizational communications and weave together a story, whether it is the right one or not. If the wrong story takes hold, it can be devastating to a culture, even if it isn't true.

    For example, a health system had many enthusiastic communications about a new multimillion-dollar research building, which was fully funded by a grant from the state. At the same time, the organization had a financial crisis from increased staffing costs and was not able to approve clinician raises. The external grant-funding for the building could not have been used for salaries. Regardless, the perception was that the organization was prioritizing buildings over people. While that wasn't true, the dots that people (inaccurately) connected did a lot of damage to morale. People felt leadership didn't care about them, only about growth. What could have been exciting news—new resources coming into the system—was met with hostility.

When you follow these tactics, you can move communication from sporadic to random to consistent and unified. The more people hear the same messages at the same time, the better they will understand what they need to do, the less anxious they will be, and the more effective your organization will become.

COMMUNICATION IS A TWO-WAY STREET

It's important to limit the use of one-way communication. One-way communication means that the sender of the message communicates but that there is no mechanism for feedback or response from the receiver. Organizational communication can often feel like an announcement on the radio—you hear it, but there is no way to respond. If one-way communication is used too much, it can send the message to employees that "your voice doesn't matter" or "the decision is already made—we don't care what you think." Most leaders want to listen to people, but sometimes employees are reluctant to speak up.

Start with a question. As leaders, our instinct may be to jump into problem-solving mode and start talking, but it's often better to hit the brakes and listen first. Questions encourage active participation and engagement. They build rapport and trust and foster psychological safety. By asking good questions, we can get a feel for what's going on with our team and how they might react to what we've got to say. It shows we truly care about their thoughts and ideas.

Questions with "yes" or "no" answers won't get us very far. Arming leaders with thoughtful questions makes it easier for everyone to have rich and meaningful conversations. People may reveal information that allows the leader to view an issue in a whole new way or to discover an issue (work related or personal) that the leader can help solve.

See the following section for a few conversation starters. Sometimes, playing with wording until you find a question that works well for you can make all the difference.

CONVERSATION STARTERS

Asking people how they are, what they need, and what you can do for them shows them you care. Good questions help you get the information you need to be a better leader. Never assume you already know. Here are a few trust-building questions to ask during rounding and at other times. Pick a question or two that you like and start there.

- ***What worries you the most?*** **(Don't assume you know.)** The book *Wonder Drug: 7 Scientifically Proven Ways That Serving Others Is the Best Medicine for Yourself* shares some research from the University of Colorado School of Medicine. When researchers asked emergency department (ED) patients, "What worries you most?" they received all sorts of answers they didn't expect. In fact, researchers found that patients' biggest worries matched the complaint that brought them into the ED only 26 percent of the time. If patients aren't asked about their biggest worries, then dangerous underlying conditions such as addiction or depression can go undetected and unacknowledged.[4]

    We can also transfer this to a work team. Ask your direct reports, "What is your biggest concern or worry right now?" This accomplishes so much. It is part of open and honest communication. It helps create that critical sense of belonging. It also reduces anxiety because it allows the leader to work with the team member on some next steps.

- ***What matters to you?*** The Institute for Healthcare Improvement suggests using this question to help deliver personalized care to patients, but it can be equally effective when communicating with caregivers.[5,6] This allows us to think about how to craft our messaging and address unique and individual needs. Remember $N = 1$ (see chapter 5).
- ***How can I support you in your role? What does support from me look like?*** This helps show genuine interest in employees' needs and lets you know when assistance is needed.
- ***What do you find most rewarding about your work?*** If you are looking for people to recognize (see chapter 6), this question is great for figuring out where an employee likely excels.
- ***What challenges are you currently facing in your work?*** This question demonstrates that leaders care about team members' well-being and success. It may also uncover needs they have, such as additional training and development, new equipment, or additional staffing.
- ***What ideas or suggestions do you have for improving our processes or workplace?*** As we discuss elsewhere, asking for employee input shows you value their expertise. Since they are closest to the action, they might also be in the best position to find solutions.
- ***What are your professional goals, and how can I help you achieve them? Are there additional training or resources to which you'd like to have access?*** These questions show that you're committed to the person's growth and development. This is so important to the current generation of talent (see chapter 12).
- ***How can we create a more inclusive and diverse work environment?*** Letting people know that a respectful and supportive workplace is a priority for you is a huge trust-builder.

Ask the Golden Question

Below is a letter from Eric Connell, who is a hospital CEO. He shares that he has gotten great results now that he's started saying, "I work for you. What do you want me to work on today?" He went on to write:

> Both times I have asked that question it has led to real and meaningful conversations that have energized me.
>
> First, in the cafeteria, a team member answered that I could go into the back and help unload the truck. I met the manager and another team member back there and put large cans of green beans away and shuttled broken-down cardboard boxes. That action created a space for the manager to share a challenge that she was having with our hiring process, which was too slow, and which I was learning of for the first time.
>
> This morning I was walking through the clinic to catch up with my practice manager. I stopped and said, "Good morning" to one of the nurses. When I tried your question, she paused for a second, and then opened up and shared a frustration she had with me. We had chatted several weeks ago, and she was upset because we didn't have a meeting like we had talked about having as a follow-up to our conversation. She was correct. We had talked about getting together to talk but had not followed through. I offered a sincere apology and pulled out my phone, and we both looked at our calendars and found a time for next week.
>
> That question is golden, and I plan to wear it out as I learn to be a more effective and sincere leader.[7]

Try this "golden question" with your employees. Don't be afraid to ask it. Leaders tend to worry that people will ask for something they can't give or that they'll hear really bad news, but usually that's not the case. Quite often the employee will bring up something you *can* fix, and you'll end up getting a quick win. If you hadn't asked, you would never have had the chance.

Don't worry if asking the question feels awkward at first or if you get an unenthusiastic response. Don't give up. Keep asking. The more you practice, the more natural it will feel.

All of these questions are part of what we call Relationship Rounding. This is a practice that allows leaders to build a solid relationship with each person and figure out what that person truly wants and needs. It also allows leaders to identify red flags that could indicate well-being issues. When people are busy or overwhelmed, it is easy for rounding to move from a practice of listening and building relationships of trust toward a transactional "checking a box" exercise. Relationship Rounding helps us get back to the original intent of rounding.

These conversation starters can be extremely powerful. Getting people talking is only part of the equation. It's also important to listen to the answers in a way that helps you get to the root of employee concerns, make them feel heard and valued, and strengthen your relationship with them.

USING COMMUNICATION TO BUILD GOODWILL AND POSITIVITY

Good communication isn't just about sharing information, instructing, seeking feedback, and coaching and correcting. It's about doing these things in a way that builds goodwill, improves morale, and creates a healthy, positive work environment. The following section offers a few tips.

Make Time for Positive Communication

Sometimes leaders have to deliver difficult messages, and the skills to do so are really important. But people crave positive communication as well. They want to be reminded of their purpose and value on the team. For each criticism of an employee, many positive comments are needed for an employee to feel good about a leader. It's ideal for leaders to begin most conversations with a positive, ask whom should be recognized while rounding, and send thank-you notes.

It is so important to master the skill of holding positive conversations to create a workplace that is energizing and enriching, makes people feel valued and cared for, and creates a true sense of belonging. Here are some tips for holding positive conversations:

- **Hold up the mirror.** Are you bringing positive energy with you to each situation or sucking energy from others? Pay attention to how people behave after an interaction. Do they seem energized, inspired, and productive? Or do they seem emotionally drained?
- **Don't guess at how people feel.** When talking with those you lead, be very specific. Ask them whether they feel appreciated by you. They will likely say yes. If so, ask what you are doing to make them feel that way. This will help you do more of it in the future. (If they have trouble giving you an answer, it might be time to ask yourself why.)
- **Make positive communication part of every meeting.** For example, start by telling a story that connects people back to mission and shares a win. This will shift the energy in the room and get people engaged right away. Most likely you'll get better outcomes.
- **Watch out for toxic positivity.** Toxic positivity is a focus on being completely positive, all the time. When we reject negative emotions and pretend challenges don't exist, employees can't relate to us and may not trust us. Certainly they won't feel heard and understood. They won't speak up about valid concerns (including their own mental health struggles), and they won't take risks.

- In times of crisis, people need frequency and transparency of communication, and they need to know that their fears and concerns are being acknowledged and addressed. They need a sense of "holding" and safety more than inspiration or motivation.[8] Overly positive or exuberant communication during these times can sometimes seem insensitive or out of touch. Leaders can still share a sense of hope in our ability to overcome, but it's important not to sugarcoat reality or fail to acknowledge and honor when others are feeling scared, discouraged, and uncertain.
- There's a difference between optimism and toxic positivity. Optimism is rooted in reality. We can think positively while still acknowledging challenges and hardships.

Communicate in a Way That Keeps People in Their "Upper Brain"

Michael E. Frisina, who wrote *Leading With Your Upper Brain: How to Create the Behaviors That Unlock Performance Excellence* with Robert Frisina, explains the importance of keeping people in what he calls their "upper brains," which is a state of mind in which they're creative, happy, fulfilled, and trusting. This is the state of mind where they do their best work. The opposite state is the "lower brain." When people are in their lower brains, they are stressed, frustrated, and driven by fear. They might follow orders, but they're too focused on keeping themselves safe to do much else.[9]

Reducing fear of a conversation's content is a helpful way to prime people to listen, converse, and absorb information. It can be anxiety provoking if you aren't sure whether you might be in trouble or not, and fear puts us in survival mode. This is especially true for those who tend to have more of a people-pleasing disposition. Vague requests such as "We need to meet ASAP" can trigger the fear center.

If you are not delivering bad news, it can help to address those fears upfront. You might say, "Everything is okay, but there is a critical operational update we need to discuss urgently." If you need to deliver bad news, give people the benefit of preparation. Instead of "we need to talk," be more specific: "A colleague has brought up some concerns about your performance. I wanted to talk with you about it in person so I can get your input on the best path forward." Nobody wants to be caught off guard.

Harness the Power of Storytelling . . .

Organizations have become very good at sharing the great work being done by their team. Storytelling helps everyone in the organization stay connected to the difference being made, which in turn keeps them tied to that crucial sense of passion and purpose. It's a great way to showcase how the organization is living its mission.

Stories are how humans have communicated since the beginning of time. Ever since humans sat around fires in caves, stories have been an important part of the way we communicate. When we tell a story, we take a single important moment in time and give it a multiplier effect. A story is like a single pebble tossed in a pond, rippling outward and touching others.

Stories are tools for helping people understand and process change. They're a great way to learn and transfer knowledge. They are how we remember things. When we can unite an idea with an emotion, we create something memorable for people, something that can be repeated.

The right story, well told, reconnects people to their passion in a way that other communication simply can't do. It helps lighten the load on days when our teams are weary. It rejuvenates us. Such a story can be a huge motivator.

Storytelling is a way to engage people on a whole new level. It helps people grasp the nuances of life not through a practical lens but on a heart-and-soul level. It turns a message into a personal and emotional experience.

When you tell a great story, you spark a connection. We love stories because we often see ourselves in them, and this helps us find commonality with others. Stories build a sense of community. We are all in this together.

. . . And Use It to Honor and Preserve the Best Parts of the Past

Stories help promote the legacy of your organization and the great people who have passed through the halls. Collecting and telling stories about the heroes on your team is a way you can thank them and honor them for the work they do.

Stories are truly the energy that can help you reignite the passion in others. If you are the one burning fiercely, seek out those who need a spark. Share the stories of those who have made a great difference. You never know whose life you'll change for the better. You never know who needed that reminder of the calling that brought them to this place.[7]

REFERENCES

1. Robison, J. 2021. "Communicate Better with Employees, Regardless of Where They Work." Gallup Workplace. Published June 28. http://gallup.com/workplace/351644/communicate-better-employees-regardless-work.aspx.

2. Rock, L. K., J. W. Rudolph, M. K. Fey, D. Szyld, R. Gardner, R. D. Minehart, J. Shapiro, and C. Roussin. 2020. "'Circle Up': Workflow Adaptation and Psychological Support via Briefing,

Debriefing, and Peer Support." *NEJM Catalyst Innovations in Care Delivery* 1(5).

3. Agency for Healthcare Research and Quality (AHRQ). 2015. "Use the Teach-Back Method: Tool #5." Updated September 2020. https://www.ahrq.gov/health-literacy/improve/precautions/tool5.html.

4. Trzeciak, S., and A. Mazzarelli. 2022. *Wonder Drug: 7 Scientifically Proven Ways That Serving Others Is the Best Medicine for Yourself*. New York: St. Martin's Essentials.

5. Barry, M. J., and S. Edgman-Levitan. 2012. "Shared Decision Making—The Pinnacle of Patient-Centered Care." *New England Journal of Medicine* 366(9): 780–81.

6. Institute for Healthcare Improvement. 2023. "The Power of Four Words: 'What Matters to You?'" Accessed September 9. http://ihi.org/Topics/WhatMatters/Pages/default.aspx.

7. Studer, Q. 2022. *The Calling: Why Healthcare Is So Special*. Pensacola, FL: Gratitude Group Publishing.

8. Petriglieri, G. 2020. "The Psychology Behind Effective Crisis Leadership." *Harvard Business Review*. Published April 22. http://hbr.org/2020/04/the-psychology-behind-effective-crisis-leadership.

9. Frisina, M. E., and R. W. Frisina. 2023. *Leading with Your Upper Brain: How to Create the Behaviors that Unlock Performance Excellence*. Chicago: Health Administration Press.

CHAPTER 8

Fairness

FAIRNESS IS ABSOLUTELY critical in building trust. It is nearly impossible to trust somebody who we believe treats us unfairly, especially if we perceive it as deliberate. One of our earliest sources of outrage as humans is the feeling that somebody or something has violated the principle of fairness. While many of us have witnessed that "life isn't fair," the frustration that comes from unfairness doesn't really go away as we get older; it just looks different.

We are social beings, which means that our interpretation of our own circumstances almost always includes an element of comparison to those around us. We are constantly assessing equity and fairness, and we adjust our behavior in response. However, just because we learn to adapt to and deal with inequity doesn't necessarily undo the damage it causes.

Lack of fairness is one of the top six drivers of burnout.[1] Our own research also has highlighted the seriousness of inequity at work. We analyzed financial strain and perceived pay-cut inequity within an organization, and we examined whether there was a relationship between these phenomena and overall employee well-being. Financial strain was not associated with overall distress, but the perceived *inequity* of pay cuts was. The issue wasn't the reduction in money; it was the feeling that it was unfair.[2,3]

If we are seeking to maximize the human margin, then an understanding of the role of inequity in both psychological and physical health is important. Perceived inequity often makes us feel lower on the social ladder. Over time, research shows that negative changes in the social hierarchy—for example, someone who was on top gets pushed down—negatively affect that person's health. Similarly, when someone of lower social status is elevated, their health is positively affected. The correlation is very strong.[4] When we are not treated fairly, we feel devalued and sometimes powerless.

Addressing sources of inequity and pursuing fairness at work are critically important for health and well-being as well as for retention. Most importantly, fairness goes together with trust. People will not trust somebody who treats them unfairly.

WHAT DOES FAIRNESS LOOK LIKE?

So what does it look like to put fairness into action? Often, we think we are being fair, but our employees and teams don't see it that way. Two key principles can support our efforts to create a fair environment.

First, we should pursue equity rather than equality. Equality and equity are different. Equality means that everybody receives the same treatment regardless of any personal characteristics or circumstances—for example, everybody getting the same-sized slice of cake at a party. Equity means that we take individual differences and circumstances into account when we allocate resources—for example, giving some people a slice of cake and having ice cream for the person on a gluten-free diet.

Second, people expect us to ensure fairness in the process *and* fairness in the results.[5] Fairness in the process means that we are transparent and fair in the methods we use to decide who gets what resources (or burdens, such as assignments to the holiday shift). Fairness in the results means that the allocation of resources or burdens takes important differences among people into consideration, resulting in a fair end result. People who complete more training or endure more difficult conditions and risk will expect a higher reward relative to others.

BE AWARE OF INPUTS AND OUTPUTS

Perceptions of inequity offend our internal desire for fairness, but they also make us feel powerless and unappreciated. The other crazy thing is that things don't actually have to be inequitable; we just have to *think* they are for the damage to occur.

Adams' Equity Theory gives us some ideas about how to think about equity and how people tend to resolve perceived inequity. The theory suggests that we constantly evaluate our ratio of inputs and outputs in relation to other people's inputs and outputs. Inputs are the amount of work, training, effort, and skill I put into something, and outputs are the rewards I receive at the end (e.g., salary).[6,7,8]

This is classic "keeping up with the Joneses" stuff, and we do it instinctively.

Here's an example. Let's assume that my neighbor has a nicer car than mine, but they are younger than me and work fewer hours, judging by the times at which they pull out of and into their driveway. I think about my inputs—how hard I work, my long hours, how long I've been in the workforce, the extra degrees I've gotten, and how much student debt was needed to make that possible. Then I think about their inputs—fewer years at work, less education, and fewer working hours. Next, I judge the outputs: new fancy car for them, older used car for me.

On the surface, I feel that I am putting in more work (education, long hours) for less reward (an older used car). This creates a sense of inequity, which is psychologically uncomfortable. As a result, I try to comfort myself by imagining that my neighbor must have old family money or that they are in deep debt but are just pretending . . . the list goes on.

People do this at work all the time.

Here are the ways we tend to try to relieve the psychological discomfort of perceiving that somebody else is putting in less and getting more out than we are:

- **Reducing inputs:** Putting in less effort, leaving work early, or doing personal things on work time
- **Trying to increase outputs:** Lobbying for a pay increase or a better job title
- **Changing perceptions:** Convincing ourselves that the other person has advantages we don't see or that we have unfair setbacks that they don't
- **Leaving:** Leaving the department, organization, or field for an arrangement that feels more equitable
- **Comparing ourselves to somebody else:** Finding a different comparison that makes us feel better about ourselves[6,7,8]

You can see how many of these behaviors could have a negative impact on engagement, retention, and productivity. Leaders and supervisors play an important role in the fair allocation of rewards and burdens, including pay and promotions, vacation time approvals, mentoring, and a shot at that highly visible project. How can we ensure fairness for our caregivers?

Give individualized consideration. One of the hallmarks of transformational leadership is the idea of individualized consideration. This means that you work to understand the unique strengths, abilities, and needs of each person and support and lead them as an individual. Making everything equal without considering people's individual inputs and outputs is likely to result in perceptions of inequity.

Ask, ask, ask. The best time to figure out whether a decision will have people yelling, "Not fair!" is before the decision is made. It is better to get input from many different voices and groups before deciding how resources or assignments will be allocated. You won't be able to please everyone, but this input will help you identify blind spots in your plan. Hearing people's reactions to different possible options can also help you figure out how to manage expectations and communicate about the decision.

Be transparent. Give people as much clarity as possible about the process, how decisions were made, and the results. We all tend to overestimate our own efforts and underestimate our rewards relative to others. Transparency helps stop the guessing game. When we can see the rationale and results clearly, we don't have as much room to assume that things are unfair.

Be mindful of favorites. We all have them. There are always those people whom we just click with and want to see succeed. Usually, they remind us of ourselves. As a result, it is easy for us to accidentally give those people preferential treatment at the expense of others whom we don't connect with as well. Be sure that you are giving everyone on your team fair treatment and opportunity. Data can help with this. If certain people are getting more of your time, more approvals, more coaching, more money, or fewer undesirable shifts or projects, you may be supporting your favorites at the expense of others. If you aren't sure, ask: "Do you feel that you are being treated fairly in our department? Do you feel that others have better support to succeed here?"

Just having a policy is not enough. Having policies and procedures about eligibility for certain benefits or consequences for poor performance doesn't mean much if the policies are not applied consistently. For example, an organization may offer paid sick time for parents to care for their sick children, but men may get more pushback than women for using that time.

Don't get paralyzed. Sometimes, we just don't have enough to go around. We may not have enough of a certain resource to help everyone, but that doesn't mean we cannot help anyone. If you don't have enough to go around, prioritize those with the greatest need or the greatest inputs and efforts. Be clear about your decision-making process and criteria and any plans to bring additional resources moving forward.

Perception is reality. In addition to pursuing fairness in our decision-making, we also have to manage *perceptions* of fairness.

People are constantly making comparisons and calculations about outputs and inputs to determine fairness, but they may not have the facts straight. Leaders can help employees make more accurate assessments by clarifying their understanding around inputs and outputs. For example, if an employee gets promoted because they work harder, have gotten extra training, and have taken on an additional assignment, those things may not be visible to their peers, who may assume that the promotion is unfair. It is up to the leader to provide clarity and transparency so that others can understand why the decision was made.

UNCONSCIOUS BIAS

"Birds of a feather flock together." We tend to gravitate toward people who remind us of ourselves and away from people we perceive as different. What is worse is that often we don't even realize we are doing it. This is called *unconscious bias*. Unconscious bias is an important concept in the pursuit of fairness. It is scary because we all have it—every human. Even the best ones. Having it is not the problem—*ignoring* it is the problem. If we don't deal with it, it affects our decision-making and allows inequity to persist in a variety of ways. Unconscious bias might manifest in the following ways:

- "He just doesn't look the part."
- "She just doesn't have 'executive presence.'"
- "I don't know if this person is a 'good look' for us."
- "I don't think they would fit in here."

These statements reflect potential biases rather than the competence or ability of the individual. When we fail to address our unconscious biases, we also reduce the diversity of our teams and miss out on the broad range of talents and perspectives that can help us get better. In most cases, diverse teams outperform homogeneous teams—diversity is good for business![9]

Furthermore, employees are prioritizing organizations that they believe support diverse and inclusive teams.[10] Employees are 4.6 times more likely to leave their organization for a similar job if they don't believe that the organization values people from various backgrounds.[11]

When we don't deal with these unconscious biases and they affect our decision-making, we are setting the stage for recurring unfairness and inequity. Without our realizing it, our biases might guide how we conduct evaluations, whom we hire and promote, who gets extra training and mentoring, and even who gets priority for time off or shift selections. This can lead to enduring discrimination and harm.

It is also important to note that some groups are more likely to experience the negative effects of these biases than others. These include people of color, women, people with disabilities, and other marginalized groups. Because of this tendency, people in these groups may feel less psychologically safe at work. This means they may not be as quick to speak up when they notice something unfair, for fear of worsening existing biases. We need to pay special attention to ensuring that we are not unfairly treating people from groups who have been historically marginalized.

Do the work. The most important part of mitigating the effects of unconscious bias is to get to the bottom of what your beliefs are, where they came from, and why you have them. When you know this, you can ask yourself in new situations, "Am I viewing things a certain way because of my own biases? How can I keep an open mind about this?" This can be a hard process. Work to build trusting and supportive relationships with people who aren't like you. They can help you gain some perspective on where your thinking might be flawed.

Look at data. Do a deep dive to understand whether certain groups are having a different experience in your team or organization. Are certain groups less likely to get promoted, take advantage of resources, or receive access to training? On your employee engagement surveys, are there certain groups that are more burned out, feel less supported, or feel less psychologically safe? If so, these are all clues that some unconscious bias might be at work. Investigate further until you get to the root of it. This also helps you distinguish between a real source of inequity and what might be a perception that needs managing.

Ask for feedback. Genuinely encourage your team to speak up and give you feedback if they see you doing or saying things that seem biased. Make sure they know that you are serious about learning and wanting to improve. Thank people who have the courage to speak up and bring things to your attention.

CONCLUSION

Believing that we have been treated unfairly can make us feel powerless or unappreciated, resulting in lower engagement, retention, and (even worse) physical and psychological health. We have to invite our teams to share in decision-making and to speak up so that we can minimize inequity and avoid making decisions out of our unconscious biases.

REFERENCES

1. Leiter, M. P., and C. Maslach. 1999. "Six Areas of Worklife: A Model of the Organizational Context of Burnout." *Journal of Health and Human Services Administration* 21(4): 472–89.

2. Meese, K. A., A. Colón-López, R. Dill, G. A. Naik, P. J. Cendoma, and D. A. Rogers. 2021. "Perceptions of Inequitable Compensation Reductions Among Healthcare Workers During Covid-19." *Journal of Health Care Finance* 48(2): 1–15.

3. Meese, K. A., A. Colón-López, J. A. Singh, G. A. Burkholder, and D. A. Rogers. 2021. "Healthcare Is a Team Sport: Stress, Resilience, and Correlates of Well-Being Among Health

System Employees in a Crisis." *Journal of Healthcare Management* 66(4): 304–22.

4. Marmot, M. G., and R. Sapolsky. 2014. "Of Baboons and Men: Social Circumstances, Biology, and the Social Gradient in Health" in *Sociality, Hierarchy, Health: Comparative Biodemography: A Collection of Papers*, edited by M. Weinstein and M. A. Lane (eds.). Washington, DC: National Academies Press.

5. McFarlin, D. B., and P. D. Sweeney. 1992. "Distributive and Procedural Justice as Predictors of Satisfaction with Personal and Organizational Outcomes." *Academy of Management Journal* 35(3): 626–37.

6. Borkowski, N., and K. A. Meese. 2020. *Organizational Behavior in Health Care*. Burlington, MA: Jones & Bartlett Learning.

7. Adams, J. S. 1963. "Towards an Understanding of Inequity." *Journal of Abnormal and Social Psychology* 67(5): 422–36.

8. Adams, J. S. 1965. "Inequity in Social Exchange," in *Advances in Experimental Social Psychology*, vol. 2. Amsterdam: Elsevier.

9. Hunt, V., S. Dixon-Fyle, S. Prince, and K. Dolan. 2020. *Diversity Wins: How Inclusion Matters*. McKinsey & Company. Published May. http://mckinsey.com/~/media/mckinsey/featured%20insights/diversity%20and%20inclusion/diversity%20wins%20how%20inclusion%20matters/diversity-wins-how-inclusion-matters-vf.pdf.

10. Lean In. 2022. "Women in the Workplace: 2022." Accessed August 27, 2023. https://leanin.org/women-in-the-workplace/2022/the-state-of-the-pipeline.

11. Mylod, D. 2022. "Three Ways Equity Impacts Healthcare Performance." Press Ganey. Published April 14. https://info.pressganey.com/press-ganey-blog-healthcare-experience-insights/3-ways-equity-impacts-healthcare-performance.

CHAPTER 9

Autonomy

In 1875, the famous British poet William Ernest Henley wrote a poem called "Invictus," which ends with the lines, "I am the master of my fate, / I am the captain of my soul." This passage captures the deep human desire for autonomy and a sense of control. Even before young children can form longer sentences, parents often hear the phrase "No! I do it!" as their toddlers try to assert their independence. Whether you tend to be a rule-follower or a maverick, the desire for at least some degree of autonomy is within you from birth.

Giving people a sense of autonomy at work is an important way to show that we trust them and to increase their trust in us in return. The quest for autonomy has been studied for many years as a substantial motivational factor for people. Dan Pink's model of motivation suggests that humans are motivated by autonomy, mastery, and purpose. Maslow's hierarchy of needs, a popular framework for human motivation, identifies autonomy as a core element of self-actualization.[1,2,3] Lack of autonomy is also one of the top drivers of burnout.[4]

In our own research, autonomy kept showing up. A sense of autonomy was consistently in the top five things that predicted better well-being[5] and was important for employees to be willing to recommend an organization. It was also related to lower turnover intentions in physicians and nurses.

In many industries, organizations have embraced flexible working options, hours, and locations. As a result, people have more autonomy in their schedules, settings, and even wardrobes (Zoom clothes on the top, pajamas on the bottom). Part of the shift toward working remotely and demanding flexible schedules stems from this desire for autonomy. It is not just about saving time on the commute or having flexibility; it is about having the freedom to exercise control over your location and daily schedule.

Because healthcare is a 24/7 operation that occurs at a specific location (wherever the patient is), the autonomy that we see in other industries is just not feasible. To ensure safety practices and meet extensive regulatory standards, many of the daily routines in healthcare leave little room for individual choice. Caregivers need to show up at a specific time and place, stay until the shift ends, wear matching scrubs, wash their hands a specific way, and shave their beard to get a good N-95 seal.

We don't believe that caregivers want autonomy any less than most humans, only that given the nature of the industry, it is harder for them to get.

If humans are motivated by autonomy, mastery, and purpose, then healthcare has some challenges. Healthcare is doing amazingly at purpose. In our research, 89 percent of caregivers, both clinical and nonclinical, say their work is meaningful.[5] Other industries would love to have that number. People choose healthcare because they feel it is a calling.[6] Opportunities for mastery also are plentiful, with years of training and practice required to master the complex skills of care delivery. Autonomy? Not so good. This will make the industry less attractive. Although the other two elements provide a strong counterbalance to the lack of autonomy, it is still a barrier to attracting talent to the field.

That means we should be diligent about maximizing autonomy wherever we possibly can. Some things are nonnegotiable and always will be for patient safety. But can we rethink shift designs to allow people to lengthen or shorten their day when they need the flexibility? Can we give employees a voice in helping shape the decisions that affect their work? Can we encourage people to trade tasks so that everyone gets more of what they want?

Wherever we *can* offer autonomy, it is a great benefit for our people.

JOB CRAFTING

Perhaps you have heard the adage "Nobody cares about your career as much as you do." Job crafting is a tool to reposition us (both leaders and employees) as active participants in shaping our work environment. It is a follower-led process that seeks to improve the fit between a person's skills, passions, and interests and the job they have. It is good for the individual, gives people a sense of autonomy and control, improves well-being and engagement, and is good for the organization.[7]

Consider two physicians who engage in a combination of telemedicine and in-person patient visits. One loves telemedicine because they save time on their commute and get to drop their kids off at school in the morning. The other dislikes it because they miss the face-to-face interactions with patients that bring them joy in their work. Both physicians can get more of what they enjoy by trading tasks; there is no net impact to productivity for the organization.

Job Demands-Resources theory suggests that motivation, well-being, and engagement result when a person has the resources needed to meet the demands of the job.[8] This equilibrium can be broadly reached in two ways: increasing resources or reducing demands.

Increasing Resources

Let's take a moment to explore the importance of increasing resources in setting the stage for engagement. Having the right resources is key to achieving excellence in our work. These may include physical, structural, and social resources.[9]

- **Physical resources.** People cannot do their work without the supplies and properly functioning equipment needed to deliver excellent care. Supply chain disruptions and drug shortages pose a huge challenge. While there are workarounds for some of these shortages, they cause additional frustration for the worker who is tasked with expending extra mental energy and time managing the workaround, adjusting policies, and managing expectations of patients regarding the changes.
- **Structural resources.** Structural resources are individual attributes or organizational aspects of the job that may help achieve work goals or support personal growth. They include a well-designed organizational structure, clear chains of command, leadership development training, career ladders, and individual autonomy. Structural resources may also include programs like counseling, on-site childcare, or workout facilities.
- **Social resources.** Social resources refer to the interpersonal connections needed to succeed at work. These may include good supervisory relationships, peer support from coworkers, and a sense of belonging. Efforts to increase social resources may include formal peer-support programs, mentoring programs, and social work events such as nurse's week or team dinners.

Without the right physical, structural, and social resources in place at all the right levels, employees face tremendous strain in trying to meet the demands of the job. This strain can lead to disengagement and burnout, which can persist for some time. Working with limited resources over long periods leaves a residue of strain and stress on the employee even years later.[10]

Certain supply chain issues or financial challenges may mean that increasing physical resources is just not possible. The great news is that you can work on increasing social and structural resources, many of which are free. Autonomy is free, and it works wonders.

Reducing Demands

Just increasing resources won't get us where we need to go. It's also crucial to think about reducing unnecessary demands.

We know that heavy workloads are difficult and that challenges in the labor market make full staffing a challenge. If there aren't enough hands for the work, the pace is very demanding. If we can't hire more people, the other way to reduce the workload and reduce the demands of the work is to make it more efficient. Over time, new technologies, new processes, and various documentation requirements from different regulators can quickly balloon into a heavy administrative burden.

If you want to know how to make the work more efficient, ask your people—they are the ones doing the same tasks over and over. In our research, we asked caregivers whether any processes or systems were redundant or unnecessary. We got over 3,000 recommendations. The things that seem like small inefficiencies, such as a few extra clicks in a software system, start to become larger problems when they are repeated hundreds or thousands of times. While inefficiency itself may not be a top driver of distress and turnover intention, heavy workload and burnout are. We can lighten the load by reducing friction in the work that results from a lack of wiggle room in unnecessary tasks.

There are a few key areas where we can focus our demand-reduction efforts on inefficiency:

Reducing duplicative documentation. Unfortunately, because of many documentation requirements that are required by accrediting bodies, local governments, state governments, federal-government funding agencies, and payers, the documentation burden often continues to get heavier and heavier. At a conference, one hospital was talking about how they provided very simple documentation for an accreditation standard. Another hospital was shocked to hear that they had been spending so much time and effort on highly detailed documentation for the same accreditation standard. The more we can reduce and align reporting to easily provide information for multiple purposes, the better.

Optimizing our use of technology. Improving healthcare technology is crucial. Electronic health records (EHRs) were expected to make healthcare delivery more efficient, but poorly designed systems that lack integration have instead added to clinicians' and caregivers' workload. With separate systems for documentation, imaging, scheduling, messaging, billing, and more, the lack of communication among these systems results in friction and workarounds. Primary care physicians are spending more time documenting and interfacing with EHRs than connecting with patients.[11]

We talked about the importance of meaning and purpose in work and how they protect against turnover intention. It's hard to stay connected with that meaning and purpose if you are spending more time looking at a computer screen than you are looking at your patients. And patients don't like it either, frankly. Consider the use of scribes or other documentation support to help relieve the burden on clinicians. Be extremely cautious when adding any new documentation requirements to ensure they are absolutely necessary.

Setting boundaries. We also need to establish boundaries and norms about how people will manage the many competing demands on their time. One example is the patient portal messaging feature. Patients have gotten more comfortable using the patient portal feature to ask their caregivers questions. These messages can quickly spiral out of control, and clinicians can feel overwhelmed with the need to respond quickly and the fear that they might miss something urgent embedded in a message. The amount of time spent outside of patient care hours in the EHR and the number of inbox messages is statistically associated significantly with increased burnout.[12] Having boundaries for patients and managing their expectations about appropriate uses for the portal and reasonable response times can help protect the patient and the clinician.

Getting clear on who is doing what. Having unclear guidelines around everyone's responsibility on the team is another area that creates inefficiency in work. When groups don't have a clear idea of where handoffs occur and of who is responsible for what, the result is duplicate work or wasted time because of problem-solving and communicating around unclear guidelines. Ideally, we are trying to avoid these two phrases: "I thought *you* were doing that" and "I already *did* that."

We want to be sure that the right person is accomplishing each task or responsibility. The ideal situation is that each person spends their day on activities that represent the highest and best use of their time and talents. We want physicians to spend their time doing (and billing for) things that only a physician can do. You don't want to overpay somebody with more qualifications to be doing a task for which they don't need their expertise. That is an expensive way to get things done.

A highly productive surgeon left his organization because he couldn't get approval to obtain some administrative support. This meant that after a full day of operating, he would spend his time printing cards and letters to his referral physicians in town, stuffing envelopes, and licking and stamping them. He is a humble guy and never felt that the work was below him but rather that it would be better for the organization if he could do one more case instead. Using a surgeon is an expensive way to make sure the envelopes get licked.

Addressing inefficiency is a way to earn and build trust with employees and patients. Inefficiencies frustrate caregivers, but they also frustrate patients. In fact, in a survey of nurses who identified increasing rates of violence and mistreatment from patients and their families, the top causes of the violence and frustration were changing policies (such as new visitor requirements) and frustration with staffing.[13] We also saw in our own research that mistreatment of healthcare workers by patients increased when there were rapid changes in workflows and policies.[14] Inefficiency is linked with violence and mistreatment.

The more effort we can put into reducing inefficiencies and redundancy now, the better off we will be. Process improvements don't just improve the life of caregivers and their satisfaction with work; they also yield results for a long time. Fixing one broken process might save hundreds or thousands of hours of work for many people for many years.

As Dr. Melinda Aston so eloquently puts it in her article on the topic: "Get rid of stupid stuff."[15] In her organization, a program designed to "get rid of stupid stuff" has saved over 1,700 nursing hours per month across the health system. Wow!

INCREASING CHALLENGE DEMANDS

Wait—increasing demands is a good thing? Not all work demands are bad. The challenge demand is a task that feels hard but results in a sense of pride and accomplishment when it gets done. Tackling a challenge demand gives people a sense of accomplishment and expands their skills.

When a person is disengaged, it might not be burnout but rather boredom. In this case, the issue can be addressed not by taking things off an employee's plate but by giving them a challenge demand that might reinvigorate them for the work. If somebody is getting to the place where they've hit their stride, maybe they don't feel stretched anymore. Sometimes the way to bring them out of a state of apathy or disengagement is not to remove demands but to provide a challenge demand. This might be a new project or assignment to lead a new initiative or take ownership of mentoring new employees in the organization.

The research shows that people who job-craft to pursue new challenge demands fare better than those who simply try to reduce demands.[16] If a person is disengaged, it might not be that the job is too hard but rather that it is too mundane: boredom, not burnout.

EMPOWERING LEADERSHIP

We want our employees to actively job-craft. The work still gets done, and everyone is happier doing it. When caregivers feel supported to job-craft within their current roles, they are less inclined to leave for a better fit elsewhere.

Empowering leadership is a style of leadership that focuses on creating self-leaders rather than followers. This involves encouraging independent action and setting goals together.[17] The aim of empowering leadership is to support followers in becoming their own leaders, which leads to improved alignment with organizational goals, increased autonomy, and enhanced trust. This style of leadership results in improved engagement, commitment, job satisfaction, and a sense of control and confidence, which ultimately leads to improved well-being.[18] Empowering leaders display the behaviors shown in exhibit 9.1.

Exhibit 9.1. Traits of an Empowering Leader

Empowering Leader Behavior	What Right Looks Like
Fosters participation in decision-making	• Involves me in important decisions • Makes many decisions together with others • Asks me about decisions that will affect others
Expresses confidence	• Believes that others can handle difficult tasks • Believes in the growth potential of employees • Expresses confidence in others' ability to perform at the highest level
Enhances the meaningfulness of the work	• Helps others understand how their objectives and goals relate to those of the organization • Helps others understand how their job fits into the bigger picture
Provides autonomy for the work	• Makes others' work more efficient by keeping the rules and regulations simple • Allows others to do their jobs their way • Allows others to make important decisions on their own if there is a need to act quickly

Source: Data from Audenaert et al. (2020).

HOW TO EMPOWER EMPLOYEES TO JOB-CRAFT

Employees may have many ideas about what would help them enjoy their work more while making the best use of their skills and talents, but they might need "permission" to do so. Here are some questions you can ask to get the conversation started around job crafting:

- What are the elements of your job that make you feel energized and engaged? Is there a way we can get you doing more of that?
- What kinds of tasks or activities drain your energy at work? Is there anyone else on the team who might enjoy those things or see them as a growth opportunity?
- What inefficiencies do you see in our current activities? Do you have ideas on how to fix that? Would you like to lead the effort?
- What is something that you think would challenge you but that you would enjoy learning how to do?

Once you have this conversation with each member of the team, you can identify tasks that could potentially be reallocated to bring everyone more joy in their work. For example, if one person enjoys doing reporting and analysis but doesn't like talking to customers, while another person loves human interaction but hates using Excel, it might be time for a trade.

CONCLUSION

Humans have a deep need for autonomy, but healthcare has strong obstacles to it. Empowering leaders recognize this need for autonomy and seek to maximize it for the people they lead. Empowering leaders can help increase autonomy and improve job satisfaction, engagement, and well-being by actively encouraging their teams to job-craft.

REFERENCES

1. Pink, D. H. 2011. *Drive: The Surprising Truth About What Motivates Us*. New York: Riverhead Books.

2. Hackman, J. R. and G. R. Oldham. 1974. *The Job Diagnostic Survey: An Instrument for the Diagnosis of Jobs and the Evaluation of Job Redesign Projects*. New Haven, CT: Yale University Department of Administrative Sciences.

3. Maslow, A. H. 1943. "A Theory of Human Motivation." *Psychological Review* 50(4): 370–96.

4. Maslach, C. and M. P. Leiter. 2022. *The Burnout Challenge: Managing People's Relationships with Their Jobs*. Cambridge, MA: Harvard University Press.

5. Meese, K. A., A. Colón-López, J. A. Singh, G. A. Burkholder, and D. A. Rogers. 2021. "Healthcare Is a Team Sport: Stress, Resilience, and Correlates of Well-Being Among Health System Employees in a Crisis." *Journal of Healthcare Management* 66(4): 304.

6. Studer, Q. 2021. *The Calling: Why Healthcare Is So Special*. Pensacola, FL: Gratitude Group Publishing.

7. Slemp, G. R., M. L. Kern, and D. A. Vella-Brodrick. 2015. "Workplace Well-Being: The Role of Job Crafting and Autonomy Support." *Psychology of Well-Being* 5(1): 7.

8. Bakker, A. B. and E. Demerouti. 2007. "The Job Demands-Resources Model: State of the Art." *Journal of Managerial Psychology* 22(3): 309–28.

9. Tims, M., A. B. Bakker, and D. Derks. 2012. "Development and Validation of the Job Crafting Scale." *Journal of Vocational Behavior* 80(1): 173–86.

10. Meese, K. A., L. M. Boitet, K. L. Sweeney, L. Nassetta, M. Mugavero, B. Hidalgo, R. Reamey, and D. A. Rogers. 2023. "Still Exhausted: The Role of Residual Caregiving Fatigue on

Women in Medicine and Science Across the Pipeline." *Journal of Medical Internet Research*. Published June 14. https://www.jmir.org/2023/1/e47629.

11. Stein, C. M. 2015. "Academic Clinical Research: Death by a Thousand Clicks." *Science Translational Medicine* 7(318): 318fs49.

12. Dyrbye, L. N. 2023. "Relationships Between EHR-Based Audit Log Data and Physician Burnout and Clinical Practice Process Measures." *Mayo Clinic Proceedings* 98(3): 398–409.

13. Incredible Health. 2022. "Study: 34% of Nurses Plan to Leave Their Current Role by the End of 2022." Published March 16. http://incrediblehealth.com/blog/nursing-report-covid-19-2022.

14. Meese, K. A., A. Colón-López, A. P. Montgomery, L. M. Boitet, D. A. Rogers, and P. A. Patrician. 2022. "Rules of Engagement: The Role of Mistreatment from Patients in the Nurse, Physician and Advanced Practice Provider Experience." *Patient Experience Journal* 9(2): 36–45.

15. Ashton, M. 2018. "Getting Rid of Stupid Stuff." *New England Journal of Medicine* 379(19): 1789–91.

16. Harju, L. K., J. Kaltiainen, and J. J. Hakanen. 2021. "The Double-Edged Sword of Job Crafting: The Effects of Job Crafting on Changes in Job Demands and Employee Well-Being." *Human Resource Management* 60(6): 953–68.

17. Pearce, C. L. and H. P. Sims Jr. 2002. "Vertical Versus Shared Leadership as Predictors of the Effectiveness of Change Management Teams: An Examination of Aversive, Directive, Transactional, Transformational, and Empowering Leader Behaviors." *Group Dynamics: Theory, Research, and Practice* 6(2): 172.

18. Audenaert, M., B. George, R. Bauwens, A. Decuypere, A. Descamps, J. Muylaert, R. Ma, and A. Decramer. 2019. "Empowering Leadership, Social Support, and Job Crafting in Public Organizations: A Multilevel Study." *Public Personnel Management* 49(3): 367–92.

CHAPTER 10

Well-Being

A CRITICAL COMPONENT of trust is the feeling that your organization and leaders care about you as a person. It is a lot easier to feel this way when you believe that your mental and physical health are supported in the workplace.[1] Employee well-being has been thrust into the spotlight over the last several years. Suddenly, it's part of the leader's job description. They are being asked to recognize the signs of mental health issues and direct struggling employees to the resources that can help. This is a totally new responsibility for most, and very few have the skill set to help in this area.

This is not only important because caring for employees is the right thing to do; it also makes a huge difference in current and future performance because of how our brains work. When we sense a threat, the part of our brain that is used for creativity, strategic thinking, and higher-level decision-making shuts down. The part of our brain that reacts quickly without thinking kicks in. If you have ever been in a high-intensity fear situation and reacted poorly, somebody might have asked later, "What on earth were you thinking?" The truth is that you weren't—that part of your brain was in the back seat.[2,3,4,5]

The pressing fears of predators have now been replaced by other sources of fear, many of them in the workplace: gossip, aggression, discrimination, or job insecurity. Yet in many ways our survival feels no less threatened. Our brains and bodies are well adapted to help us run if we see a lion, but we are not as equipped to endure constant stress.

When we endure continued stress over long periods of time, the structure and functioning of our brains can actually start to change. The parts of our brains that are responsible for higher-level thinking can begin to atrophy, while the parts of our brains used for reactivity and aggression become enlarged.[2] This means that over time, we become less able to make good decisions and more reactive. This really puts an exclamation point on the importance of reducing sources of distress and creating healthy work.

The good news is that with development, leaders can catch issues early and make a big difference in employee well-being. They are in a good position to notice when something is wrong and identify mental health issues early before they escalate. They are a major resource for helping people get through tough times. Leaders may not be able to fix many of these issues for employees, but they can start the conversation and get things moving in the right direction.

This is not an optional issue. Patient outcomes are at stake. Staff well-being and engagement are connected to the patient experience, which in turn is linked to clinical outcomes. And issues such as burnout are highly contagious. When doctors and nurses are emotionally exhausted, others around them catch it.[6] If we know that pockets of burnout exist, we need to address them as soon as possible. There is no next generation of healthcare workers if the current ones are not healthy.

Prioritizing employee well-being fits the mission of every organization.

Of course, levels of burnout and other mental health issues can vary widely from one organization to another and from one person to another. Your organization might be better than some and worse than others. The only way to know is to measure these levels. Many simple, validated measures can be used to get an idea of where the organization's well-being is. These questions may be addressed through existing employee engagement survey vendors, or you may need to measure independently. By looking at the variations across departments, divisions, and roles, you can identify hot spots that may be in greater need of an intervention.

People need a way to privately measure and assess their own state of well-being. Many apps and survey tools, some of which are free, can support people in doing this. If people can track their progress over time, they can identify when they may need more support and what things in their lives are affecting well-being.

KNOW THE DIFFERENCE BETWEEN STRESS, BURNOUT, AND TRAUMA

Why do managers need a working knowledge of these conditions? Because stress, burnout, and trauma each require a different set of responses.

Stress is a term for the way an individual responds to events or circumstances. It is a physical, mental, or emotional strain. In small doses, stress is actually helpful. It motivates us, makes us productive, and adds excitement to life. But when stress gets to be too much or goes on for prolonged periods of time, we can have physical and emotional symptoms: fatigue, headache, upset stomach, high blood pressure, irritability, anxiety, and depression. Chronic stress over long periods of time can affect the size, shape, and functioning of our brains, making us more reactive and less able to use higher-level reasoning and make strategic decisions.

Certain types of stress over time can lead to *burnout*. Psychologist Christina Maslach describes burnout as having three dimensions: emotional exhaustion, cynicism, and a feeling of ineffectiveness.[7] When someone is burned out, they're not just exhausted temporarily. They're exhausted all the time. A good night's sleep or a vacation won't fix the problem. Their performance suffers. They make more mistakes. They've stopped being able to see that their work has purpose and that they make a difference.

Trauma is a whole different level of stress. Experiencing or witnessing a traumatic event can send us into survival mode. It makes us feel threatened, and it changes how we look at the world. Typical acute stress after a traumatic event lasts for around a month, while trauma symptoms can last for months or years. People can experience trauma from what they witness happening to others (such as a patient), not only from things that directly happen to them. There are four main signs of trauma:

1. **Reliving the event.** Intrusive or unwanted thoughts of the event can happen spontaneously throughout the day, when triggered by a memory or certain noises and smells, or through nightmares.
2. **Avoiding things that remind them of the event.** For example, if somebody experienced the trauma of a car crash, they may avoid driving. Clinicians have reported being triggered just by walking into the hospital after witnessing a tragic and traumatic patient death, and they may have trouble returning to the same unit or floor. This might manifest as being late or disengaged, when in fact it is a trauma response.
3. **Having more negative thoughts and feelings than before.** People may experience loss of pleasure in things they previously enjoyed, numbness, or feelings of fear or anger more often.
4. **Feeling on edge.** You may notice that people are irritable, seem to startle easily, or get agitated. This is called hyperarousal, and it is a side effect of trauma.[8]

It is so important to recognize how serious a person's issue is so that we can direct them to the right kind of help. With stress and burnout, we can probably direct the person to internal resources. However, trauma usually requires a more complicated intervention.

Employees experiencing trauma may benefit from trauma-informed leadership. People want five things from their leaders when they are experiencing trauma:

1. Hear me
2. Protect me
3. Prepare me
4. Support me
5. Care for me[9]

HAVE THE TALK: EXTENDING HELP TO EMPLOYEES IN DISTRESS

Recognizing that an employee is in distress and then responding appropriately is a complex but important task. Consider the following steps when engaging in such interactions.

Look for signs of distress. Some warning signs of distress in employees may be visible to you as a leader:

- An unusually short fuse
- Withdrawal or isolation
- Unkempt appearance or exhaustion
- Emotional outbursts or tearfulness
- Worsening relationships
- Decreased performance or absenteeism

If you notice these signs, make it a point to have a check-in. Don't assume that these signs are only performance related—there might be a root cause of distress or trauma.

Don't avoid conversations about well-being. Sometimes managers may suspect that something is not right with an employee but may not know how to start the conversation. Yes, these conversations can be awkward, but they are a part of the job now. Don't think of them as "difficult conversations" but as "caring conversations." Train yourself on them. It is important to help managers build this skill set. Role-playing can help a lot. The more we practice something, the more comfortable it becomes.

Help employees develop their understanding. It may help to provide an educational session, video, or article on what well-being, stress, and trauma look like. Remember, not all stress or trauma affects everyone the same way. We know that people experience stress differently. Some people bounce back easily when they face crises or tough times. Some don't. They may struggle to varying degrees, and some may move into trauma.

The simple chart shown in exhibit 10.1 can be used as a conversation starter for employees to discuss their well-being. It identifies specific symptoms that individuals may be experiencing and helps them pinpoint whether they need assistance. Many healthcare professionals are private by nature and reluctant to seek help. It may be helpful to give this chart to employees and let them assess themselves. (Also, be on the lookout for these red flags in yourself.)

Let people assess where they are on the spectrum. There are varying degrees of mental health issues, from stress to burnout to trauma. These issues need to be addressed in different ways. (Also,

Exhibit 10.1. Creating Safe Environments for Conversations

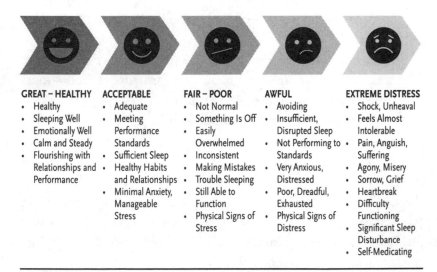

GREAT – HEALTHY	ACCEPTABLE	FAIR – POOR	AWFUL	EXTREME DISTRESS
• Healthy	• Adequate	• Not Normal	• Avoiding	• Shock, Unheaval
• Sleeping Well	• Meeting	• Something Is Off	• Insufficient,	• Feels Almost
• Emotionally Well	Performance	• Easily	Disrupted Sleep	Intolerable
• Calm and Steady	Standards	Overwhelmed	• Not Performing to	• Pain, Anguish,
• Flourishing with	• Sufficient Sleep	• Inconsistent	Standards	Suffering
Relationships and	• Healthy Habits	• Making Mistakes	• Very Anxious,	• Agony, Misery
Performance	and Relationships	• Trouble Sleeping	Distressed	• Sorrow, Grief
	• Minimal Anxiety,	• Still Able to	• Poor, Dreadful,	• Heartbreak
	Manageable	Function	Exhausted	• Difficulty
	Stress	• Physical Signs of	• Physical Signs of	Functioning
		Stress	Distress	• Significant Sleep
				Disturbance
				• Self-Medicating

assessment is a great conversation starter. Sometimes people don't realize how much they are affected by stress.)

Open the door. Even if employees realize that they are in distress, they may not feel comfortable talking about it. Ask for their permission to initiate a conversation about well-being. You might say, "Your well-being is very important to me, and I've noticed you seem more stressed than usual lately. Can we have a conversation about how you are doing?" If the person isn't ready to talk yet, let them know that you will be there if they change their mind later and that you want to support them. If you notice violent tendencies, self-harm, or other dangerous behaviors, this conversation is no longer optional.

One person might say, "Well, I'm calm and steady. I'm able to take things in stride. I feel I'm able to communicate effectively." This person falls into the "Great-Healthy" category.

Someone else might say, "I'm more easily overwhelmed and irritated. I'm having trouble eating and sleeping well. I'm getting headaches." This employee is moving into "Fair-Poor" or even "Awful" territory, and it is starting to affect their physical health.

Others may confess they're starting to self-medicate, feeling fatigued and exhausted, and having panic attacks. These folks may have moved into "Extreme Distress" and likely need added support and professional help.

You may even have a few employees who are having thoughts of self-harm or suicide, are easily enraged or aggressive, or are making dangerous mistakes. If so, you need to take immediate action. This may include mandating their participation in an Employee Assistance Program (EAP) or walking them to the emergency room.

Respect your limits. You're not there to judge or to diagnose. You *are* there to let people know you care about them and to direct them to resources if needed. If someone came to you and said, "I have blood in my urine," you would say, "You know what, we have great physicians here who can help you. Let me help you get an appointment." Mental health issues are no different.

It is so important to catch issues such as stress, burnout, or trauma early. Many people are such committed professionals that they will hold things together at work while things at home suffer. Sometimes work is the last place where suffering manifests. By the time it shows up at work, the rest of the employee's life is probably in shambles. People will sacrifice in other areas of their lives to continue to perform at work. As long as they are able to keep their job, they still think they are doing okay, and they're probably not going to speak up.

You never know who is checking in on your employees outside of work. You may be the only one noticing their signs of distress. It may feel uncomfortable, but just ask. It can make a huge difference in the lives of others.

A HELPFUL TOOL: THE "BATTERY-CHARGE" QUESTION

The battery-charge question is one way to help people feel more comfortable with sharing their concerns and to build open and honest communication. Jay Kaplan, MD, shares that in his role as chief medical officer he was often in patient care areas. He would ask the staff, "How are you?" He would usually get an answer such as "fine" or "good." Later he would hear a sad story about a staff member, which showed that although they said "good," in reality they were not good at all. He realized he needed to try something different.

That's when Dr. Kaplan thought of the smartphone. Think about how a person treats their phone compared to how they treat themselves. They buy a protective cover for it. They keep it safe. They don't let it get too hot or too cold. And they work hard at keeping it charged. So he asked staff to think of themselves as phones. With that in mind he started asking, "What is your battery charge right now?" Instead of hearing vague answers like "good" or fine," he heard numbers like 80 percent or 50 percent.

Healthcare people are good teammates and want to be helpful. This practice led to the people with higher battery-charge numbers wanting to help those whose battery charge was lower. It led to both a group conversation and individual conversations. Leaders who use this tactic find that it helps them determine whether the issue is a work item or something else.

At times the question can reveal a more serious issue and create an opportunity to share resources that are available. Healthcare organizations often provide more resources for well-being, including mental health assistance, than most other businesses. The challenge is lack of use. Dr. Kaplan and the organization created material that went with the battery check.

There have been so many wins from this question! It also allows us to position the organization well in providing so many well-being avenues. And it demonstrates that we are interested in employee concerns and that those concerns can be discussed in an open and honest fashion.

The battery-charge question can be powerful. In a workshop practicing this question, one person said to Quint, "I'm a zero." Nobody had said this before; usually if someone is struggling, they will fudge it a little bit and say they are maybe a 40 or 50. After this, Quint shared his own alcoholism recovery story with the rest of the group. But he didn't forget about the "zero" lady, and went to look for her at lunch.

He said, "Tell me about the zero." She said, "I'm sort of a role model for recovery here. People bring me up when someone is in recovery. Well, during the pandemic, I've relapsed. And I don't know what to do." By that afternoon she was getting the help she needed. If we didn't do the battery checks, she would probably have said, "I'm fine."

There is power in saying something out loud. Good conversations can be incredibly healing. We all have triggers, which set off these "inner tapes" that play in our heads. When we say them out loud to a safe person, it can give us some needed perspective. We discover that the tapes we're playing aren't the healthiest of messages.

Become a resources expert. Know your numbers. As discussed, the whole point of well-being conversations is to direct people to the resources they need. In healthcare, we're fortunate to offer great benefit packages and a variety of user-friendly mental health and well-being resources. Lack of resources is usually not the problem. It's that only a small percentage of individuals use them. We recommend that CEOs monitor on a monthly basis how many employees are accessing resources. Typically, between 1 and 3 percent of the employees use resources related to well-being, self-care, or mental health. In fact, many times this number is 1 percent. The challenge is creating the environment where people feel safe to access these resources.

Leaders, give your resources a test run. One organization recommended that every physician take part in the mental health services as part of their residency program. Why? Because if everybody goes, it will encourage those who want to go but are afraid to. And those who may not really need the services will at least know what they're like when they recommend them to patients—or if they or a family member ends up needing mental health services down the road.

Get to people early. A chief nursing officer (CNO) mentioned that one of her best nurses quit. She was stunned. She called up the nurse and said, "You've quit? I thought you loved being a nurse." The woman said, "I do love being a nurse." She went on to tell the CNO about a family situation she was experiencing. Later, the CNO said, "If I had only known, we could have intervened earlier and may not have lost that nurse." Sometimes we wait too long with mental-health issues, and we lose good people. The earlier you can help, the less they will be affected by long-term chronic stress and trauma, which can harm our bodies and brains.

Prioritize reducing the stigma. Mental health is stigmatized in many professions but particularly in health care. Healthcare tends to be a "just get over it" culture, and people can be rather stoic. They have a misunderstanding of resiliency—it doesn't mean to ignore the pain, push through, and suck it up. They also don't want to be perceived as weak, so they suffer in silence. Many are concerned about privacy and confidentiality issues. Sometimes they have to be treated in the same hospital that they work in.

A big part of getting employees the help they need is to make it very clear that it is not only okay but also expected and urgent to let you know when they are struggling. Let them know it's safe to ask for the care they need without negative consequences or jeopardy to their careers.

Reassure people they are not alone. When you are going through hard times, you think you are the only person in the world who has a problem. It can be extremely lonely. Once people start to share, they find that many people have similar problems. When Quint shares his history of recovery (see the sidebar), people often reach out and share their own struggles with addiction.

Leaders, it's okay to be vulnerable. Just saying, "It's okay to speak up" may not always be enough. A huge part of breaking the stigma is modeling the behavior we want to see. Leaders need to go first. We need to talk openly about our own issues. This creates the psychological safety others need to share their own truth. It also reassures people that they are not alone, which is incredibly comforting.

Sometimes leaders are reluctant to share their own stories. They think it goes against the image of what a leader should be. But it's a myth that people want to follow strong, undefeated leaders. The truth is the opposite: People really appreciate vulnerability in leaders.

Over the years, both of us have shared stories about our own struggles, sometimes against the advice of others, and have never regretted it (see sidebar). We have found that it opens doors for connection and empathy for others who are struggling.

Some people are private by nature. But the reality is, other people usually know something is going on. They just don't know what. When there's an information void, people will fill it with speculations and worst-case scenarios. If a leader is clearly experiencing a personal difficulty, they may benefit from sharing about it to keep employees from discussing it among themselves. This doesn't mean to give every detail. It does mean letting them know you're struggling. Not only will this stop the gossip, but it also helps them feel closer to you and strengthens your relationship.

In His Own Words: Quint's Journey to Recovery

Growing up, I never felt like I fit in. I was sort of a square peg in a round hole. So when I tried my first beer as a young teen—maybe around 14 or 15—I felt I had found the solution. When I was drinking, I didn't feel as depressed or sad or afraid. I continued, mostly binge drinking, throughout high school.

I got married young and had two children while in college. I wanted to be a good father, so that kind of gave me some "guardrails" and kept me in line for a while. But when I was 26, my wife and I divorced. After that I started living the proverbial double life. I was still drinking and at the same time working hard to get my master's degree and to show everyone that I was good enough, though deep down inside I felt that I wasn't.

Then I ended up remarrying, and my wife suggested I use my employer's EAP. I did, and I went to the psychologist who told me, "There's a 90 percent chance you're an alcoholic." My response was to feel relieved that I was in that 10 percent! (Denial is part of the disease.) After that, I did what I call a recovery "drive-thru," which lasted about three weeks before I relapsed again.

Then, on December 25, 1982, I woke up and had a moment of clarity. I realized that something was really wrong. By that time I'd had a couple of failed marriages, my cars were being repossessed, and I was grocery shopping at convenience stores so I wouldn't run into people I knew. I realized that if I didn't change, I was going to kill myself. So I went to see a minister who convinced me to get healthy.

From there I went to see a therapist. I remember the day the light went back on. She told me, "Quint, I notice when I tell you something critical, you let it in and tell me eight more things wrong with you. But when I give you positive feedback, you deflect it. Maybe the reason you feel so negative about yourself is that you filter out all the positives."

That was a big "aha" moment for me. I walked out of there, and I just felt different somehow. (This was spring of 1983.) I had finally realized that we need to look at what's right as much as what's wrong. And this is a truth I've shared for years in my work. We in healthcare tend to be hard on ourselves—and we need to start being kind to ourselves.

So that is my recovery journey. Forty years later it is still going on. And that is why I care so much about EAPs, mental health, and being open about the struggles all of us face.

Remind people to be kind to themselves. Humans have a negativity bias, in which we tend to skim over the positive and focus on the negative. We look only at what's wrong, almost never at what is right. We all do this at times. In healthcare we're hard on ourselves, but self-compassion is crucial. If there's one piece of advice that applies to everyone, it is this: Be kind to yourself. Don't beat yourself up.

Reconnect people to purpose. From time to time, we all get worn down and maybe even a little burned out. We have a string of hard days (or weeks or months) and lose sight of what we're doing and why we're here in the first place. This is normal. The good news is that at times, a simple reminder can completely change our outlook.

Here's a great activity for shifting mindsets that can be used in department or team meetings, training sessions, or any kind of gathering, really. Ask everyone to think about these two questions and share their answers with the group:

1. Why did you choose to work in healthcare?
2. You could work anywhere. Why do you choose to stay at [insert organization name]?

It's amazing to see how these two questions reconnect people to mission. They remind us of the difference we make and everything that we can be grateful for. The energy in the room shifts, and it makes for a more positive, productive meeting or session.

There's another great by-product as well. When leaders hear all the reasons people like working at their organization, it fills the leaders' cups, too.

Ask these questions often. You'll love the good feelings it creates, and you'll help people get in the habit of thinking about their jobs in a different way.

CREATING HEALTHY WORK

As we discussed in chapter 3, one of the most surprising findings of our research was that of all the different stressors at work and at home during the COVID-19 pandemic, the ones predicting overall distress were almost all work related. Similarly, burnout is specifically defined as an occupational phenomenon.

The following six factors drive burnout:

*   **Workload:** an overwhelming amount of work to be done in a limited amount of time
*   **Control:** a lack of control over the work that is being done, including decision-making authority and autonomy

- **Reward:** a lack of recognition and reward for hard work and achievements
- **Community:** a lack of supportive social connections in the workplace, including feelings of isolation and exclusion
- **Fairness:** a perception of unfair treatment, favoritism, and bias in the workplace
- **Values:** a conflict between personal values and the values and mission of the organization.[10]

Any improvement in these areas is going to make a big difference in terms of supporting the well-being of our workforce.

Job Demands-Resources theory[11] suggests that well-being occurs at the balance of the demands of the job and the resources to meet those demands. This means that you can attempt to get to that state of well-being in two ways: increasing resources and decreasing demands.

Our research continues to show that both sides of the equation are important in mitigating distress. Resources such as autonomy, meaning, training, and appropriate supplies are important. It is also important to reduce demands such as heavy workloads, long hours, inefficiency, inequity, and conditions that create moral distress. This data also tells us that *just* providing resources will never get us there. This is why many organizations provide EAP services, counseling, gyms, vacation time, and well-being training but do not see the movement they need in employee well-being.

We can't always ease workloads and hours by hiring more people. However, we can work to address redundant and inefficient processes and non-value-added tasks. An intervention called Getting Rid of Stupid Stuff (GROSS) involved employees in identifying inefficiencies and systematically eliminating them. In doing this, the organization saved 1,700 nursing hours per month, which will reap benefits for hundreds of months to come![12]

Just ask. Employees probably already have many ideas about how to improve the processes they see daily. However, they need to be empowered to raise those solutions and ideas. Leaders can develop a structure for listening to and getting feedback from employees on how to improve the efficiency of the work by eliminating unnecessary tasks, using new technologies, and streamlining processes.

Widen the net. Sometimes suggestions for improvement and efficiency will come from unlikely places. Make sure to give all employees, not just those with more powerful or visible positions, an opportunity to voice their ideas. Physicians, environmental services, food services, nurses, managers, and students are all observers of the system and may have valuable insights. You can also seek patient input. Patients often spend many hours in waiting rooms or hospitals beds watching our processes. They likely have some suggestions about efficiency too.

Be careful of how you spend efficiency gains. When we improve a process and see gains in our efficiency, the tendency is to "spend" these gains by adding more patients or activities to improve the financial margin. This happens often in process improvement projects. We reorganize the clinic flow to reduce unnecessary walking and use the saved time to add a couple more patients. We need to be sure that we are spending some of those gains on making workload and pace more sustainable. If we improve efficiency but our clinicians still don't have time to eat or go to the bathroom during their shifts, it doesn't help us make progress on the human margin.

Shaping employees' work lives is not easy. That's why leadership is a skill set, one that's important to master. No one is born knowing how to lead. And few are able to pick it up when they become interim leaders, as people in healthcare so often do.

Great leadership takes investment, and plenty of it. Creating the conditions that create a culture of wellness is an integral part of that training. Every leader behavior, every tactic, every process, and every procedure that goes into creating a well-run organization either supports that wellness or detracts from it.

We owe it to our clinicians and staff—and, of course, our patients—to create high-performance organizations where people can be healthy and supported at work.

REFERENCES

1. Leiter, M. P., and C. Maslach. 2000. *Preventing Burnout and Building Engagement: A Complete Program for Organizational Renewal*. Hoboken, NJ: Jossey-Bass.

2. Fuchs, E., and G. Flügge. 2003. "Chronic Social Stress: Effects on Limbic Brain Structures." *Physiology & Behavior* 79(3): 417–27.

3. Savic, I. 2015. "Structural Changes of the Brain in Relation to Occupational Stress." *Cerebral Cortex* 25(6): 1554–64.

4. Chow, Y., J. Masiak, E. Mikołajewska, D. Mikołajewski, G. M. Wójcik, B. Wallace, A. Eugene, and M. Olajossy. 2018. "Limbic Brain Structures and Burnout—A Systematic Review." *Advances in Medical Sciences* 63(1): 192–98.

5. Frisina, M. E., and R. W. Frisina. 2023. *Leading with Your Upper Brain: How to Create the Behaviors That Unlock Performance Excellence*. Chicago: Health Administration Press.

6. Herrando, C., and E. Constantinides. 2021. "Emotional Contagion: A Brief Overview and Future Directions." *Frontiers in Psychology* 12: https://doi.org/10.3389/fpsyg.2021.712606.

7. Maslach, C., and M. P. Leiter. 2006. "Burnout." In *Stress and Quality of Working Life: Current Perspectives in Occupational Health*, edited by A. M. Rossi, P. L. Perrewé, and S. L. Sauter, 37, 42–49. Charlotte, NC: Information Age Publishing.

8. National Center for PTSD. 2023. *Understanding PTSD and PTSD Treatment*. US Department of Veterans Affairs. Published August. http://ptsd.va.gov/publications/print/understandingptsd_booklet.pdf.

9. Koloroutis, M., and M. Pole. 2021. "Trauma-Informed Leadership and Posttraumatic Growth." *Nursing Management* 52(12): 28–34.

10. Leiter, M. P., and C. Maslach. 1999. "Six Areas of Worklife: A Model of the Organizational Context of Burnout." *Journal of Health and Human Services Administration* 21(4): 472–89.

11. Demerouti, E., A. B. Bakker, F. Nachreiner, and W. B. Schaufeli. 2001. "The Job Demands-Resources Model of Burnout." *Journal of Applied Psychology* 86(3): 499–512.

12. Ashton, M. 2018. "Getting Rid of Stupid Stuff." *New England Journal of Medicine* 379(19): 1789–91.

CHAPTER 11

Healthy Teams and Coworker Relationships

THE WAY WE lead our teams can help or hinder how employees build trust with us and with each other. Creating the conditions to support flourishing teams lays the foundation for trusting relationships.

WHY THE WHOLE TEAM MATTERS

Healthy teams and good coworker relationships are important not just for employee flourishing but also for organizational success. Working on a healthy team serves as a kind of "psychological PPE" that can protect us against the many daily stresses of work.[1] When we unite against our common enemies of disease and injury, and strengthen and encourage each other for the battle, we can keep fighting—even when times are tough.

A peek into an operating room in a tertiary care center leaves you with one impression: healthcare is a team sport.[2] You may see a surgeon; an anesthesiologist; a certified registered nurse anesthetist; a scrub tech; a nurse; and maybe a student, resident, and fellow. Just looking at burnout or engagement for physicians or nurses misses one major factor: their experience is affected by everyone else in the room.

You can't have a happy physician surrounded by distressed, burned-out nurses. You can't have a flourishing nurse practitioner surrounded by a team in misery. That is why we need a strong emphasis on cultivating healthy teams and good coworker relationships.

SETTING THE CONDITIONS FOR SUCCESS

Our first step in setting the stage for healthy teams is to make sure we organize the work and responsibilities to minimize unnecessary friction. Practically speaking, this can be difficult because of the reporting structures in place at many healthcare organizations. Often physicians report through a specific structure, nurses report to nursing leadership, and supporting staff and managers report to other senior leaders. In many instances, the responsibility for these different areas does not converge until the C-suite. The way we structure our organizations does not always reflect the interprofessional nature of how the work is performed, which can make the process of measuring and managing the shared experience of the team quite complicated. Who really owns the task?

This lack of shared coordination and responsibility for the work can lead to role ambiguity and role conflict. These two concepts are occupational stressors that are associated with many negative outcomes.

Tackling Role Ambiguity

Role ambiguity means that I don't know exactly what I am supposed to be doing—what is my job and what isn't. It occurs when my responsibilities and degree of authority are unclear.[3] There may be a role ambiguity problem when you hear the phrase "I didn't know it was my job."

Where there is shared responsibility, there is the opportunity for role ambiguity. In healthcare, the contributions and responsibilities of each team member are not always clear. Where do the duties of the patient care technician end and those of the nurse begin? When does the nurse escalate to the nurse practitioner? Does a physician need to be involved? If so, when? These responsibilities are sometimes guided by regulations at the state level, such as scope-of-practice laws, or by differences across departments, locations, and individual physician preferences ("Dr. X lets me do this on my own, but Dr. Y wants to be in the room every time").

What is already unclear becomes even trickier when roles and responsibilities are rapidly reshuffled to work around staffing shortages. Nurses have found themselves often handling the work of respiratory therapists, food and services, guest relations, and patient care technicians.

Increased role ambiguity or scope-of-practice changes were also associated with increased distress in our 2021 data.[4] Lack of clarity about our role is associated with a number of negative outcomes that make it difficult to have healthy teams:

- Anxiety
- Burnout
- Depression
- Job dissatisfaction
- Dissatisfaction with supervision and coworkers[5]

Author Brené Brown says, "Clear is kind."[6] The leader has an important role in helping to clarify responsibilities of team members and define clear handoffs and criteria for escalation. We owe it to our people to make sure that all members of the team understand what each person brings to the table and what their role is.

Reducing Role Conflict

Role conflict involves competing, incompatible demands placed on a person. Many working parents experience daily role conflict. *How do I maintain my role as a high-performing employee and invest enough time in my children? Say yes to the speaking engagement or go to my kid's soccer game?* In the workplace, many healthcare workers have dotted-line reporting structures and unofficial bosses. Consider the nurse in the operating room. The surgeon wants one thing, and the nurse manager wants something different. How do I please both? This is role conflict. It is stressful! That's why research has shown that role conflict[3] leads to

- overall job dissatisfaction;
- dissatisfaction with work tasks, supervision, coworkers, pay, and growth opportunities;
- low organizational commitment and job involvement;
- turnover intention; and
- poor job performance.

The more we can collaborate across silos and clarify expectations and processes, the better chance we have of reducing role conflict. To get an idea of whether your employees are experiencing role conflict, you might ask them, "Whom do you feel like you need to please to do a good job at work? Which people do you interact with who have expectations for how you do your job?"

FOSTERING PSYCHOLOGICAL SAFETY

Creating a psychologically safe environment is also critical for supporting healthy teams. Psychological safety is "a shared belief held by members of a team that it's OK to take risks, to express their ideas and concerns, to speak up with questions, and to admit mistakes—all without fear of negative consequences. As [Dr. Amy] Edmondson puts it, 'it's felt permission for candor.'"[7]

Psychological safety doesn't mean that people can say whatever they want whenever they want with no consequence—there can still be expectations for professionalism and civility. However, it does mean that all voices are welcome at the table and that everyone is respected and encouraged to speak up and to contribute to decision-making. It also shows up often in our own research of things that increase the odds of recruiting and retaining employees. People want to work in an environment where their ideas are valued or where they at least feel that they are allowed to contribute to the conversation.

Some things shut down psychological safety quickly. Someone starts to speak, and before they can get the thought out or explain their idea, another person says, "That will never work," "We tried that before, and it never worked," or "We've always done it *this* way." This tells people that it's not safe to bring up a new idea or to fully consider it. If certain people in the room don't agree with the idea, it will get shut down.

Psychological safety also means that we can share ideas or feedback without fear that it will be used later in a negative way. If ideas that are shared are ridiculed in closed-door meetings behind my back, or in a gossiping situation, we no longer feel safe.

SUPPORTING HEALTHY COWORKER RELATIONSHIPS

Leaders can't guarantee that people will become close friends, but we can create conditions that support strong bonds between coworkers and colleagues. When people know how to be good coworkers, these kinds of friendships are more likely to form. Even if they don't, an organization full of good coworkers and strong peer relationships shines in every possible way.

Social connections at work matter. For years, Gallup has been looking at the effects of having a best friend at work and has found that having a best friend at work is more important now than it was before the pandemic. Gallup notes that those who report having a best friend at work are more likely to

- engage customers and partners,
- get more done in less time,
- support a safer workplace,
- innovate and share ideas,

- have fun on the job,
- recommend the employer, and
- intend to stay.[8]

Good relationships at work do so many things for the individual and the organization. People tend to be more engaged, motivated, and committed to meeting goals and supporting the organization's mission. They are more likely to trust others, and communication improves. Change is less painful when people can lean on one another to navigate the uncertainty.

All of this improves productivity and performance. Coworkers are more generous with their time and share knowledge, skills, and expertise with one another. There's a free exchange of ideas. People are willing to provide valuable feedback, advice, and mentorship. All of this bolsters professional development and creates a culture of continuous learning and innovation.

Strong relationships also mean there's less toxic behavior like gossip, bullying, blame, and competition. This allows leaders to spend less time managing drama and more time on productive tasks. When conflict does arise, it can usually be settled quickly. Stronger relationships generally foster understanding and compromise.

The whole culture gets better, stronger, healthier, and more inclusive. People feel a powerful sense of belonging and connection, which reinforces their engagement and commitment to the organization and one another. All of these factors together create conditions that make it easier to attract and retain top talent. High performers want to work with other high performers, resulting in less turnover and a more stable workforce.

WHAT A GREAT COWORKER LOOKS LIKE

Based on people's past experiences both inside and outside work, they may not have seen what great coworker relationships look like in action. Great coworkers exhibit the following qualities:

- **Accountability: do what you're supposed to do.** Accountability encompasses a range of behaviors, such as being on time, meeting deadlines, and cleaning up after yourself. It's all about respecting the time and space of those who work with you. Great coworkers don't make excuses.
- **Good work ethic.** People appreciate hard workers, and they definitely notice those who are the opposite.
- **Collegiality.** This involves creating harmonious relationships characterized by a sense of shared responsibility and respect for each other. Great coworkers bring issues to a person directly rather than going around them or talking behind their back.
- **Honesty.** Great coworkers don't lie, mislead, manipulate, or steal credit from others. If they make a mistake, they admit it.
- **Helpfulness.** When people are overwhelmed, great coworkers step in to help. If they're having a slow day, they offer to lighten the load for someone else. They may offer to teach a new skill or a better way of doing things. They may offer to mentor new coworkers.
- **Optimism/positive attitude.** Great coworkers don't complain. They are pleasant and courteous. They focus on the positive. Rather than being a drainer, a great coworker seeks to spread positivity.
- **Good communication.** Being able to write and speak clearly is important, especially when collaborating with others. It's also important to answer emails in a timely fashion. Each job connects to so many others.
- **Humility and openness to feedback.** No one wants to work with a braggart or a know-it-all.
- **Adaptability.** Change can be really hard. Great coworkers set a good example for others by managing their own reaction to change and finding ways to help others who might be struggling with a new direction.

Of course, this is just a partial list. Most of us know what a good coworker looks like if we've been fortunate enough to have one. The vast majority of people want to do a good job and get along well with peers and colleagues.

Spell Out What Right Looks Like with Standards of Behavior

When people are on their best behavior, they communicate more clearly, there are fewer unpleasant conversations, and everyone enjoys work more. Collaboration, innovation, and consistency improve. It all adds up to more engaged employees, improved performance, and happier patients.

It is helpful for the team to adopt norms of behavior—a set of expectations for how they relate to one another. Consider spelling them out, giving specific examples, and including them in a formal Standards of Behavior document. Unless you spell out what good behavior looks like, not everyone may know. That's why developing a formal Standards of Behavior contract is so powerful. It clarifies everything, from interactions with clients and customers to the details of how we behave toward leaders and coworkers.

Ideally, team members will be part of the process of creating these standards to increase buy-in and adoption. Everyone needs to be involved in developing the contract. You can use the list of good employee behaviors in the previous section as a starting point. Ask leaders and employees alike to share their ideas. Then put them all together in a final document and have everyone sign it. Put it somewhere visible.

A few helpful tips:

- Be specific in your wording. Don't write, "Be polite to coworkers." Instead, write, "Say thank you when someone helps you" or "Say good morning when you pass someone's office as you arrive each day."

- Before you finalize the document, give employees the final sign-off. This makes buy-in a lot more likely.
- Explain the reasoning behind the standards when you roll them out to everyone. Connect the standards to your mission, vision, and values.
- If someone violates a standard, hold them accountable. This probably means just reminding them what the document says on the issue. Most people want to do the right thing, but we all are human.
- If you violate a standard, admit it and apologize.
- Treat the Standards of Behavior as a living document. Change it as needed.

TOOLS AND TACTICS FOR FOSTERING GREAT COWORKER RELATIONSHIPS

Make sure that people are the priority. One of the biggest obstacles to good coworker relationships is an overemphasis on tasks and an underappreciation of relationships. This gets worse in high-pressure environments and is why you might have employees who are excellent producers but who don't spend the time to foster good relationships. They are so focused on getting the task done that they don't think through how their approach may damage relationships. Make sure your team knows that the way they care for their colleagues, not just getting the task done, is an important part of their performance.

Understand and appreciate differences in people. Make sure you recognize and appreciate the differences you have among your team members. When people feel that their unique talents, skills, and personalities are valued on the team, they are less likely to feel the need to compete with their colleagues for recognition. It may be helpful to conduct formal assessments to help team members appreciate the various strengths and personalities everyone brings to the table. Helpful tools include DiSC and StrengthsFinder.

Set the right example. Like it or not, employees are always watching leaders. That's why it is so important to behave in ways we want them to emulate. We can model positive, respectful, inclusive behaviors ourselves. We can step in and help with tasks when needed. We can show gratitude and say thank you.

Use training to shore up "good coworker" skills. For example, offer training sessions focused on communication, conflict resolution, having difficult conversations, or team building. The idea is to equip employees with tools and techniques to improve relationships while also giving them a shared language around these issues.

Nix the gossip. Gossip is communicating information about a person without their knowledge. Negative gossip is interesting because it affects the target of the gossip a bit, but it damages the gossiper more! It's the ultimate backfire. Gossipers have worse well-being, engagement, performance, and supervisor relationships.[9] Negative gossip is also linked with worse organizational outcomes. Allowing a negative gossip culture to persist can wreak havoc on individuals, teams, and performance. Gossip cannot be tolerated. Make this expectation clear.

Emphasize mission, vision, and shared goals. Always be looking for ways to connect people back to their calling, mission, and purpose. Communicate a clear, shared purpose that unites team members and fosters a sense of collective responsibility for the team's success. For example, start meetings with a story about how the team's work made a difference in a patient's life.

Create a culture of honesty, trust, and psychological safety. When people trust their leaders and one another—and feel safe enough to speak up without fear of backlash—they're more likely to share their concerns, ideas, and honest feedback. If people are not willing to be vulnerable, they won't build trust with one another. Without trust, good teamwork is impossible, and authentic relationships can't grow.

Be fair. It is critical to correct workload inequities and deal with low performers. There is a tendency to "work around" low performers by giving more to your high performers. When workloads are imbalanced, with tasks and responsibilities unequally distributed among team members, people notice. It leads to frustration, resentment, and even burnout—none of which lend themselves to good coworker relationships!

Find ways to get people from different departments together. One method is to initiate cross-functional projects that encourage collaboration between different departments or teams. Another is job rotation and shadowing. The idea is to expose employees to diverse perspectives and experiences. By allowing them to experience different roles or work with various team members, you help create empathy and better understanding of coworkers' responsibilities.

Encourage collaboration. The more opportunities that people have to work together, solve problems, and innovate, the more likely they are to form strong bonds. It's important to make sure that everyone gets a chance to participate and that collaboration is valued more than individual success.

Make sure that everyone's voice has a chance to be heard. This means promoting diversity and inclusion. Everyone needs to feel valued. Make it easy for everyone to contribute. Be mindful that different personalities may need different ways to participate. Some people may feel comfortable speaking up in group meetings, while others need more time to reflect and gather their thoughts privately before sharing. Create a variety of ways for people to contribute their ideas.

Have fun together. Create ways for people to connect and have fun. This tactic builds relational capital. These could be informal gatherings, lunches, games, friendly competitions, or sharing traditions. They could involve employee resource groups that bring together individuals with shared interests or backgrounds. All of this enhances camaraderie, support, and networking among employees. Be mindful that events outside of work may be difficult for those with caregiving responsibilities. Don't assume that these people are unengaged or uninterested in bonding with the team if they are not able to attend outside of work.

When we can create strong, connected, collaborative teams where people feel they belong, we find that employees are willing to do a lot for their coworkers. Even in the toughest circumstances, they will keep pressing forward. They will find a way together. Once that kind of culture is in place, it can change everything for your organization.

PEER SUPPORT

Lastly, teaching people how to provide effective peer support (and being able to provide it yourself) is critically important. Our own research shows that between 10 and 25 percent of our caregivers are experiencing symptoms of compassion fatigue, post-traumatic stress disorder, and moral distress.[10] Humans need support to process these things. It is unlikely that we will have enough licensed mental health professionals, counselors, and psychiatrists to meet the overwhelming need as a society. Unfortunately, even if it were available, some caregivers are resistant to seeking formal help because of the associated stigma. In the absence of professional help, peer support is the next best thing.

The person who truly comprehends the stress you experience at work is the one who works alongside you every day. Shared experiences hold immense value. Caregivers often feel isolated because people in their personal lives and communities fail to grasp the reality of witnessing routine tragedies in healthcare, particularly at the bedside. In fact, caregivers may hesitate to share their stories with their support networks, fearing that they would burden others with the trauma. As we mentioned earlier, even hearing the details of someone else's trauma can be a distressing experience. The things healthcare workers witness can be so deeply upsetting and disturbing that they worry that sharing them with individuals outside healthcare would only inflict additional trauma, which is something nobody wants to do.

Humans require social connection, and we know that mutual feelings of vulnerability and shared stress can often create some of the strongest social bonds in situations like this. Supportive colleagues can make a huge difference in day-to-day well-being and also in the recovery process afterwards.

Building Blocks of Good Peer Support

So how do we provide quality peer support?[11]

Look for the signs. Look for signs of distress in colleagues, such as an uncharacteristically short fuse, withdrawal or isolation, an untidy appearance, or exhaustion. You may also notice absenteeism, reduced job performance, worsened mood, deteriorating relationships, frequent tearfulness, or unusual outbursts. If you notice these signs, make it a point to have regular check-ins with colleagues. By doing this you are establishing a relationship of trust and care, and these people are more likely to feel safe about being vulnerable regarding what they are going through and what support they need.

Say something. Speak up genuinely, expressing concern with statements such as "I'm worried about you; you seem more stressed than usual. Is everything okay?" To foster trust and create a safe space, move beyond superficial inquiries and openly share your own challenges. Avoid oversharing, but be vulnerable so that people are more likely to feel safe in sharing their own experiences.

Follow up and follow through. If you promise to do something, make sure to follow through, whether it's a call or a check-in. Additionally, inquire about the best way to support your coworkers whether they need help with problem-solving, resources, or simply a listening ear.

Turn off the vent. Avoid venting and encourage sharing instead. Venting may provide temporary relief, but studies suggest it can lead to increased anger and unconstructive expressions of stress in the long term.[12]

Be vulnerable. Promote a culture of vulnerability, especially in leadership roles, by sharing your own feelings. Normalize seeking therapy and support wellness activities.

No judgment. Listen without judgment, offering a nonjudgmental ear to those struggling with mental health concerns. Avoid imposing solutions or making the conversation about yourself. Simply sit with your coworker, express care, and let them know they are supported.

Laughter and gratitude. Find moments of laughter and express gratitude. Humor can be a valuable coping tool during stressful times, so share funny stories appropriately. Thank your coworkers when they do something to help you out or make the day a little bit easier. Gratitude is a real win-win for employees. It makes them feel appreciated and noticed and helps you both feel more connected to your workplace community. Expressing gratitude doesn't just make the other person feel better; it is good for us, too. Research has repeatedly found that routinely expressing gratitude is connected to better emotional health and well-being.[13]

Don't be silent. Lastly, just say something if somebody opens up to you; don't be silent. You might say something like the following:

- "Thank you for coming to me. I am honored that you would trust me with your story."
- "You're not alone."
- "What can I do to help? Would you like problem-solving or do you just need someone to listen right now?"
- "What does support from me look like right now?"

Making Peer Support Part of the Culture

To cultivate a culture of peer support, let's explore the Circle Up model—an innovative approach that is easy to implement at the unit or clinic level and shows great promise based on initial research.[14] The best news? It is free.

Briefing huddle. Circle Up starts with a short briefing huddle at which the entire care team—including physicians, nurses, administration, and staff—gathers for a concise morning meeting. During this huddle, the team talks about what to expect for the day. Topics may include staffing shortages, difficult patients, or a new process (for example, "We are two nurses short today—how do we want to handle this?"). This is also a great time to introduce new team members, travelers, or students.

Micro-empathy. Throughout the day, team members conduct informal check-ins with one another—small and deliberate acts of micro-empathy. These interactions provide an opportunity to intentionally inquire about one another's well-being and to offer support. For example, you might say, "Hey, getting moved to a new unit with a new team is tough. How are you doing? Is there anything I can help you figure out?" These acts of micro-empathy build strong relationships over time, promoting overall well-being.

Debriefing. At the end of the shift, there is another quick debriefing huddle to recap the day. This process gives people a small release valve to address the stress of the day so that they can put it down rather than carrying it home. There is open discussion about the day's events, sharing successes and challenges. The goal is to identify areas for improvement and ensure a more successful tomorrow. During the Circle Up debriefing, you may ask questions such as "What were your reactions today?" or "What helped us work together as a team today?" Take time to do a "victory lap" and celebrate the small wins of the day. This is a great time to let people quickly offer recognition to one another to make sure they go home feeling appreciated.

Critical success factors. For the Circle Up model to succeed, consider several key factors:

- Ideally, the sessions are brief, visible, and scheduled at a time that minimizes workflow disruption. Try keeping them to 5 to 10 minutes, max.
- Acknowledge that patient care may occasionally hinder participation.
- Use recurring meetings, if available. This is preferable to introducing additional meetings.

- Leadership support is essential.
- This collaborative effort involves every member of the interprofessional team, not just physicians and nurses.

Results. By establishing regular touchpoints and prioritizing intentional empathy, we can foster a positive environment, rebuild trust, and cultivate a psychologically safe team. Initial findings on the Circle Up model's effects are quite promising:

- Improved process efficiency
- Increased agency
- Enhanced emotional support
- Improved interprofessional connectedness
- Reduced psychological distress and moral distress

Helping others feels good. Those who engaged in informal check-in behaviors experienced the personal gratification of providing assistance. The potential of this straightforward intervention is immense, and the best part is that it can be implemented immediately within your unit, without the need for higher approval. This is a low-cost, simple method to help routinize peer support and strengthen your team's well-being.

CONCLUSION

Healthcare is a team sport. We cannot thrive and flourish at work while other members of our team are burned out and suffering. Every behavior an individual exhibits builds the culture and the experience their colleagues will have. Leaders have a huge role in setting the stage for healthy teams. We can work to reduce sources of friction between colleagues and set Standards of Behavior that show employees how to create a supportive environment for one another. Peer support is more critical now than ever. You can't control other people's actions, but you can make a huge difference by creating the conditions that enable great teamwork and by modeling the behaviors of an ideal coworker.

REFERENCES

1. Meese, K. A., C. F. Dobbins, A. Colón-López, F. Van Pelt, D. A. Rogers, and K. L. Flood. 2022. "Accountable Care Team Membership and Distress: Is Accountable Care Team Membership Associated with Lower Distress During a Crisis?" *Journal of Hospital Management and Health Policy* 6(22).

2. Meese, K. A., A. Colón-López, J. A. Singh, G. A. Burkholder, and D. A. Rogers. 2021. "Healthcare Is a Team Sport: Stress, Resilience, and Correlates of Well-Being Among Health System Employees in a Crisis." *Journal of Healthcare Management* 66(4): 304–22.

3. Stepanek, S., and M. Paul. 2022. "Role Stress." Quality Improvement Center for Workforce Development. Published July 27. http://qic-wd.org/umbrella-summary/role-stress.

4. Colón-López, A., K. A. Meese, A. P. Montgomery, P. A. Patrician, D. A. Rogers, and G. A. Burkholder. 2022. "Unique Stressors in a Global Pandemic: A Mixed Methods Study About Unique Causes of Distress Among Healthcare Team Members During COVID-19." *Journal of Hospital Management and Health Policy* 6(23).

5. Örtqvist, D., and J. Wincent. 2006. "Prominent Consequences of Role Stress: A Meta-analytic Review." *International Journal of Stress Management* 13(4): 399.

6. Brown, B. 2018. "Clear Is Kind. Unclear Is Unkind." Brene Brown.com (blog). Published October 15. http://brenebrown .com/articles/2018/10/15/clear-is-kind-unclear-is-unkind.

7. Gallo, A. 2023. *What Is Psychological Safety? Harvard Business Review.* Published February 15. https://hbr.org/2023/02/what-is-psychological-safety.

8. Patel, A., and S. Plowman. 2022. "The Increasing Importance of a Best Friend at Work." Gallup. Published August 17. http://gallup.com/workplace/397058/increasing-importance-best-friend-work.aspx.

9. Wax, A., W. A. Rodriguez, and R. Asencio. 2022. "Spilling Tea at the Water Cooler: A Meta-analysis of the Literature on Workplace Gossip." *Organizational Psychology Review* 12(4): 453–506.

10. Boitet, L. M., K. A. Meese, M. Hays, C. A. Gorman, K. L. Sweeney, and D. A. Rogers. 2023. "Burnout, Moral Distress, and Compassion Fatigue as Correlates of Post-Traumatic Stress Symptoms in Clinical and Non-Clinical Healthcare Workers." *Journal of Healthcare Management.*

11. Hays, M. 2023. *Strategies for Offering Quality Peer Support to Your Healthcare Colleagues.* UAB Medicine. https://www.uab.edu/medicine/home/images/directory/strategies-for-offering-quality-peer-support-to-your-healthcare-colleagues.pdf.

12. Suttie, J. 2021. "Does Venting Your Feelings Actually Help? *Greater Good Magazine.* Published June 21. https://greatergood.berkeley.edu/article/item/does_venting_your_feelings_actually_help.

13. Jans-Beken, L., N. Jacobs, M. Janssens, S. Peeters, J. Reijnders, L. Lechner, and J. Lataster. 2020. "Gratitude and Health: An Updated Review." *Journal of Positive Psychology* 15(6): 743–82.

14. Rock, L. K., J. W. Rudolph, M. K. Fey, D. Szyld, R. Gardner, R. D. Minehart, J. Shapiro, and C. Roussin. 2020. "'Circle Up': Workflow Adaptation and Psychological Support via Briefing, Debriefing, and Peer Support." *NEJM Catalyst Innovations in Care Delivery* 1(5).

CHAPTER 12

Leadership Development

LEADERSHIP DEVELOPMENT HAS always been important. That is no different now. Many of the essential skills that help build trust with employees and teams need to be practiced and learned. Just as a surgeon practices for thousands of hours to perfect their craft, we need practice and guidance to perform at our best.

With healthcare organizations, it's not unusual to find that about 25 percent or more of people in leadership today have less than three years of experience in management. Another 20 to 25 percent may not be new to management, but they are in a new position. That means they only recently started doing tasks like budgeting, scheduling, hiring, ordering, giving performance feedback, and so forth. And many of them have little, if any, leadership training (except for watching how their leaders led).

For example, if you ask a nurse who's in a management role, "Did you attend nursing school with the idea that it is a stepping stone to being a nurse manager?" the answer is almost always "No, I went to school to be able to provide care to people." Most healthcare managers don't have a master's in healthcare administration or an MBA. If they do have a master's degree, it's usually in their technical skill. Even those with advanced degrees in leadership received them at different times from different schools. This means there can be inconsistency.

In addition to their inexperience, managers face a workplace that's more complex than ever, from new technology to staffing changes to the need to help with the well-being of those they lead while managing their own self-care.

Transactional leadership is based on processes, control, and getting tasks done. Transformational leadership is about engaging, motivating, and inspiring people to work toward a shared mission and vision. Leaders need to be competent in both. However, transformational leadership is the foundation. Without people, nothing else matters.

People want and expect professional development. Research shows that employees, particularly Generation Z employees, are more likely to stay in a position when they feel that their skill building and career development are prioritized.[1] By investing in them, you not only help them thrive in their career, but you also show them you care about them as individuals (which is also something they want from leaders).

Effective leadership development is also a huge anxiety reducer. First, it reduces the anxiety of the leaders themselves. They gain confidence as they master the knowledge, skills, and abilities to perform their jobs more effectively and efficiently. Their confidence grows as their individual performance increases and as they advance in their careers and get promotions and raises, all of which lead to greater job satisfaction. Second, leadership development reduces anxiety in other employees. As leaders become better at leading, their communication improves. They're able to convey more clearly what they need and expect from employees. This means that employees are better able to meet the needs of patients and the organization. Compliance improves. There are fewer mistakes. All of this leads to improved financial performance, organizational reputation, and patient outcomes.

The great news? A commitment to leadership development is a proven path to better organizational performance. A Gallup poll focused on the variance between high-performing and low-performing companies and found that it could be explained by the presence of strong middle managers.[2] If you can move the middle, that makes all the difference.

A NEW WAY TO THINK ABOUT DEVELOPMENT

Healthcare is constantly evolving. The industry is used to shifting processes and behaviors in response to an ever-changing external environment. Now, based on all the factors we've just discussed, it is becoming clear that it's time to change the way we develop individuals.

General, one-size-fits-all training still makes sense at times, but it does not go deep enough to create and sustain high performance. We need a new way of training that is customized to the needs, strengths, and preferences of the individual. Everyone is at a different place in their journey. They all have unique development needs. We need to meet them where they are.

By embracing a leadership development approach based on the individual, people get up to speed faster. This is crucial in a time of great disruption, economic uncertainty, and tough competition.

Another big change lies in who holds the responsibility for development. It is no longer the human resources department or a single individual that is responsible for leader development. People own their own development, and the leader to whom they report shares the responsibility to help each person develop.

Targeted, specific training with a narrow focus on outcomes is the way forward.

PRECISION LEADER DEVELOPMENT™

A process that allows for the customized development of the individual is Precision Leader Development (PLD). This method provides an approach to individual development that's similar to the way that we practice medicine.

Particularly in areas like cancer treatment, caregivers approach each patient as an individual. All humans have different genes. We live in different environments. We do different work. We have different diet, exercise, sleep, and self-care habits. We have different coping skills. As we have discussed in chapter 5, everyone is an "N of 1." One size does not and cannot fit all.

This is why precision medicine, also called personalized medicine, is needed. As the Food and Drug Administration's website explains, "The goal of precision medicine is to target the right treatments to the right patients at the right time."[3] Precision medicine takes into account all those differences in genes, environments, and lifestyles.

Similarly, PLD uses an assessment process to identify a person's strengths and opportunities based on their experience, work setting, learning style, and natural talents. *The goal of precision development is to provide the right development at the right time* to help a leader achieve their and the organization's goals.

How Precision Leader Development Works

The process starts with each person aligning their desired outcomes to the organization's outcomes. When a clear connection to the big picture of organizational goals is made, it enhances the meaning of the work. As we discuss throughout this book, meaningful work and a sense of purpose are what keep people engaged and committed when times get tough.

In the same way that precision medicine improves clinical outcomes by diagnosing each patient based on many factors, PLD looks at various aspects of a person. It uses a four-step process (see exhibit 12.1) to answer the question "How can this person best attain the needed skill?" It also helps the "one up" (the employee's immediate supervisor) better see how they can support that person in their role.

Exhibit 12.1. The Four Components of Leadership Assessment

Leadership Assessment	
Leadership Skills Assessment	Learning Style
Personality and Behavior Assessment	Problem-Solving Ability

Leadership Assessment

People tend to stay with a company when they are invested in skill building and career development. With talent development, it is important to know a person's learning style, personality, behavior, and problem-solving ability. The leadership assessment process considers the individual's potential, the skills needed in their role, and experience to create a personalized development plan that maximizes their potential.

Step 1: Leadership skills assessment. What skills does this leader have, and what do they need to do the job and achieve the desired outcomes of the role? Start with a master list of leadership skills (see exhibit 12.2) and work with the one-up (the immediate supervisor) to determine the skills that the individual needs.

Once the desired skills are selected from the master list, they are then moved to the actual assessment. First, the manager assesses themselves on a scale of 1 to 10, with 1 being *not skilled at all* and 10 being *mastery*. They then give their thoughts on the priority or importance of each skill to their role. The one-up does the same based on their views of the person. (Interestingly, people often overrate themselves despite not having outcomes to support this. This underscores the need for leaders to work on self-awareness.)

Exhibit 12.2. Examples of Foundational Leadership Skills

1. Change management
2. Selection of talent
3. Onboarding
4. Manage and reduce expenses
5. Creating revenue streams
6. Understanding financial statements
7. Running an effective meeting
8. Process improvement
9. Difficult conversations (employees, customers)
10. Talent development
11. Connecting the external environment to internal actions
12. Reward and recognition
13. Hitting deadlines, managing workload
14. Effective communication (employees, customers)
15. Creating a sense of belonging
16. Understanding and managing measurements/ metrics (HCAHPS, employee engagement)
17. Developing and editing relevant departmental/ regulatory policies and procedures
18. Technology knowledge and management
19. Conflict resolution
20. Critical-thinking skills
21. Decision-making
22. Planning, organizing, and prioritizing
23. Problem-solving
24. Continuous learning
25. Business acumen
26. Growth and development of others

This is a general list. It is important that it is tailored for each organization. Each organization's leadership team defines exactly what these skills look like inside their workplace. This collaboration and input improves buy-in and promotes the long-term success of the development program.

This exercise leads to healthy conversations about the person's self-awareness. Because the manager and their one-up will select only one or two skills to focus on at a time, it is also great for reducing anxiety. It addresses prioritization. For example, a leader may rank talent selection as important. It is. However, if that manager has a very small department with no turnover, they and their one-up will determine that this is a skill that can wait. This is a collaborative approach to development.

An organization may use a survey with master skills already filled in, like the one shown in exhibit 12.3, or may use a blank form and add specific skills tailored to the role.

Exhibit 12.3. Sample Survey: Leadership Foundational Skills Rating

Leadership Foundational Skills Rating
This survey is designed to rate your own skill level among the list below.
After you rate yourself, have your direct supervisor rate your current skill level.

Employee name:

Supervisor name:

FOR CURRENT SKILL LEVEL:
1 = Opportunity, not skilled, almost no knowledge about the subject
10 = Strength, highly skilled, could teach the subject

1. Selection of talent and onboarding

	1	2	3	4	5	6	7	8	9	10
SELF	○	○	○	○	○	○	○	○	○	○
DIRECT SUPERVISOR	○	○	○	○	○	○	○	○	○	○

2. Running an effective meeting

	1	2	3	4	5	6	7	8	9	10
SELF	○	○	○	○	○	○	○	○	○	○
DIRECT SUPERVISOR	○	○	○	○	○	○	○	○	○	○

3. Understanding financial statements, manage and reduce expenses

	1	2	3	4	5	6	7	8	9	10
SELF	○	○	○	○	○	○	○	○	○	○
DIRECT SUPERVISOR	○	○	○	○	○	○	○	○	○	○

4. Process improvement

	1	2	3	4	5	6	7	8	9	10
SELF	○	○	○	○	○	○	○	○	○	○
DIRECT SUPERVISOR	○	○	○	○	○	○	○	○	○	○

5. Understanding measurement (employees, customers)

	1	2	3	4	5	6	7	8	9	10
SELF	○	○	○	○	○	○	○	○	○	○
DIRECT SUPERVISOR	○	○	○	○	○	○	○	○	○	○

6. Difficult conversations (employees, customers)

	1	2	3	4	5	6	7	8	9	10
SELF	○	○	○	○	○	○	○	○	○	○
DIRECT SUPERVISOR	○	○	○	○	○	○	○	○	○	○

7. Talent development

	1	2	3	4	5	6	7	8	9	10
SELF	○	○	○	○	○	○	○	○	○	○
DIRECT SUPERVISOR	○	○	○	○	○	○	○	○	○	○

8. Connecting the external environment to internal actions

	1	2	3	4	5	6	7	8	9	10
SELF	○	○	○	○	○	○	○	○	○	○
DIRECT SUPERVISOR	○	○	○	○	○	○	○	○	○	○

9. Change management

	1	2	3	4	5	6	7	8	9	10
SELF	○	○	○	○	○	○	○	○	○	○
DIRECT SUPERVISOR	○	○	○	○	○	○	○	○	○	○

10. Reward and recognition

	1	2	3	4	5	6	7	8	9	10
SELF	○	○	○	○	○	○	○	○	○	○
DIRECT SUPERVISOR	○	○	○	○	○	○	○	○	○	○

www.HealthcarePlusSG.com

Step 2: How does this person best learn? Again, everyone has different needs in this area. In large group development people are presented with material aimed at a wide audience. For some, sitting in a group and listening to a speaker is okay. Others may do better with reading and participating in very small groups or individual development sessions. Identifying how each person learns most effectively is critical to maximize talents and abilities.

Awareness of learning styles acknowledges the most effective and efficient methods for transferring new skills or knowledge. Based on the learning style, the resources would be aligned for optimal results.

Step 3: What does this person need to know about their personality and behavior? The person takes a personality and behavior assessment to better understand how they respond to challenges and how they best work with others. Many tested and validated options are available online. Not only do these tools help with people in leadership, but all employees also can benefit from them. Investing in such assessments helps build teamwork and strengthen coworker relationships—both vital in retaining talent.

Recognizing and understanding one's thoughts, feelings, and behaviors is a crucial skill. Through self-reflection, individuals can learn how to make more informed decisions and foster meaningful relationships.

Step 4: Readiness for problem-solving. Here, an organization explores how each person does with critical thinking, processing information, and preparedness to engage in a process of identifying, analyzing, and resolving problems. Problem-solving allows individuals to effectively approach and address challenges. This does not mean that a person is assessed in some or all of these. It is optional and very dependent on the person and the role they have.

The organization takes all this information, processes it, and looks at it from every angle. Then through collaboration with the leader and the one-up, a development strategy can be formulated.

THE OSAR™ APPROACH

An OSAR (Outcomes, Skills, Actions, Resources) is a tool that helps leaders develop the skills necessary to execute their outcomes. The approach involves narrowing focus, establishing clarity and prioritization of key actions, and identifying the resources to achieve the desired outcomes. Outcomes, skills, actions, and resources are all considered to create an individualized development plan. Leaders and their one-ups meet monthly to review and update.

- **O**utcomes: What measurable outcomes does the individual need to achieve to meet their goal(s)?
- **S**kills: What skill(s) need to be mastered to achieve the outcomes?
- **A**ctions: What actions will the individual take to achieve the desired outcomes?
- **R**esources: What resources will the individual use to achieve the outcomes?

Exhibit 12.4 provides an example of an OSAR template.

Ultimately, each leader receives a development plan built just for them. No two plans are ever alike. This is a lot of work, but it is work that needs doing. Many of the great things we do in healthcare connect back to the presence of great leaders. And great leaders aren't born, they're shaped and developed. They're *invested in.*

One reason PLD works so well is that it's tied to execution results. The leader sees the progress they're making, which builds their self-confidence and job satisfaction. This generates the momentum needed to move the organization forward. This is a system that leaders love. With people being so busy and overwhelmed, it's critical to provide development in a way that energizes and replenishes them. They need to leave the development feeling better, not worse.

Exhibit 12.4. OSAR Template

OSAR

Name: Date:

OUTCOME	**S**KILL(S)	**A**CTIONS	**R**ESOURCES
What is the measurable outcome you want to achieve?	What skill(s) do you want to master?	What actions will you take to achieve this outcome?	What resources will be used to build these skills?
Reduce 90-day turnover from 31 percent to 20 percent.	Selection and early onboarding.	Adjust selection to new, more relevant questions.	New selection questions: • What are you looking for in your supervisor and coworkers? • What can your coworkers and I count on from you?
		Start onboarding process the minute the job is accepted.	
		Get to know the new employee better by discovering their interests, family background, and how they like to spend their free time. This helps you learn their keys to feeling, "This is the place for me."	Read *The Calling* and connect to each person's sense of place.
		Conduct weekly stay conversations.	Read article about stay interviews.
		Celebrate employee's first 30, 60, and 90 days.	

In addition, development needs to be collaborative. People want to be involved in decision-making. When they help create their own development plan, it is far more likely to be successful—and when that happens, everybody wins. Remember, people crave autonomy.

Finally, it's not about giving people more things to do but about narrowing the focus of the training, so they get highly proficient at the things they need to do their job. Remember the following:

Less = consistency = always = better outcomes

A parting note is that leadership development is not optional. It is one of the most important things we can be doing for the health of individuals and the organization. If it becomes optional, more pressing or urgent tasks will always get our attention and energy. The people who need development the most will sometimes be nervous to take advantage of optional leadership development for fear of looking incompetent. Make leadership development a priority and expectation to ensure that you have the best chance of strengthening the human margin.

REFERENCES

1. Perna, M.C. 2021. "Why Skill and Career Advancement Are the Way to Gen-Z's Heart." *Forbes*. Published March 2. http://forbes.com/sites/markcperna/2021/03/02/why-skill-and-career-advancement-are-the-way-to-gen-zs-heart/?sh=709ef61b22b5.

2. Walker, S. 2019. "The Economy's Last Best Hope: Superstar Middle Managers." *Wall Street Journal*. Published March 24. http://wsj.com/articles/the-economys-last-best-hope-superstar-middle-managers-11553313606.

3. US Food and Drug Administration. 2018. "Precision Medicine." Updated September 27. http://fda.gov/medical-devices/in-vitro-diagnostics/precision-medicine.

CHAPTER 13

Understanding Change Management

BEING ABLE TO lead and manage change well is crucial to maintaining trust. Every change brings new opportunities for misunderstanding, perceptions of inequity, and unintended consequences. All of these things can damage trust if not managed well.

WHY IS ORGANIZATIONAL CHANGE SO HARD?

Change is the norm in healthcare. It never stops. As the external environment shifts, organizations shift to respond to the changes. We all know this, and most of us accept (in theory, anyway) that we will need to regularly disrupt ourselves to avoid being disrupted by market forces. So why do so many change initiatives fall short of their goal? If they do ultimately succeed, why is there so much pushback, struggle, fear, and pain along the way? The answer is that change in healthcare is difficult because change is hard for everyone everywhere.

The overarching reason why it's so hard to make change happen is that it is more complex than expected. Leaders understand the *why* of the change, so it is easy to assume that more people are open to the change than they are. It seems logical and straightforward: We figure out the outcome we want, we draw up a plan to get us there, we figure out the necessary sequence of events, and we roll it out to the team. That works for about 40 percent of the people.

The challenge is the change process and its effect on people. This involves not just logic but emotion as well. If we don't address the powerful (and normal) human emotions that determine *why* people resist change, we will have a tough time getting them on board. (It's no secret that if they're not on board, there's little chance the initiative will be successful.) People tend to fall into three categories: those ready for change, those neutral about change, and those resistant to change.

In their heart of hearts, many people view change as loss. They believe they are about to lose something valuable. They might lose their office, their title, or their comfortable routine. They might lose their reputation as being "the smart and competent one" in their area of expertise. They might lose workplace relationships that they've come to value. If they can't master the new skills they need to master, they might even lose their job.

These losses are real and painful. We fear and resist them for good reason. In fact, adjusting to change can feel like a loss. Nostalgia kicks in: *Why can't we go back to how things used to be?* Grieving is not easy for anyone, but it's something we have to go through if we don't want to remain stuck.

Humans are wired to believe that change is difficult and threatening. As leaders, our job is to help employees believe that change will be positive, though the adjustment can be bumpy. That means providing a sense of security and reassurance that even though adjusting to change isn't easy, they will ultimately be okay—that, in fact, life will be better for them after the change.

Once they make this mindset shift, the change will be easier. A critical mass of employees "buy in" and start adapting their behavior. Once the good results start rolling in, others will join them. Eventually, everyone will begin gaining confidence as they see that they can implement the new skill or behavior, that it is working, and that—sure enough—they are okay.

Of course, the better one understands change before all of this happens, the better the implementation goes. That means we don't back off when things get rough.

WHEN TURBULENCE OCCURS, KEEP THE THROTTLE DOWN

Organizational change follows a fairly predictable path. That's a good thing because it helps leaders plan and let people know what to expect. We highly recommend reading the works of John Kotter if you'd like to learn more about change management.

Many change initiatives start off strong, then fizzle out. (You may have heard this called the "sizzle to fizzle" phenomenon.) Organizations hit a "performance wall," and things start to fall apart. This is normal. If you don't know that, you might decide to quit and move on to another initiative. Maybe a new initiative is needed, but maybe it would be better to execute on what's already underway. You won't know until you push through the wall.

The story of Chuck Yeager, the test pilot who first broke the sound barrier, is great for helping people understand the change process. To understand what he did differently, it's important to know that right before a plane breaks the sound barrier, it starts to shake like crazy. When this happened, other pilots would ease off the throttle. Chuck took a different approach. He kept the throttle down. When he did, there was a big boom (we now know this is the sonic boom), and then a smooth flight resumed.

The takeaway for leaders? When turbulence hits, don't ease off. Every time you do, the odds of success decrease. Instead, keep the throttle down.

When you realize that turbulence is not a bad thing—actually, it means you're getting closer to a breakthrough—your mindset shifts. You'll stop listening to naysayers and losing momentum. You'll work to keep people passionate and committed to meeting the goal.

It is normal to want to slow down when we feel turbulence. But in healthcare, sometimes we need to keep pushing for improvement. The stakes are high. Patients are counting on us. We have a human responsibility to keep the throttle down.

TWO BIG CHANGE DERAILERS: SEQUENCING AND LACK OF CLARITY

It is natural for healthcare leaders to want to do too much at once. They want to fulfill the mission of the organization. However, that can be counterproductive. Why? People can be successful only in incremental change. One or two changes can often be implemented quite well, but when more changes are added, success drops. In 2022, the average employee experienced 10 major enterprise-wide change initiatives, up from two in 2016. Not surprisingly, employees' willingness to support enterprise change plummeted to just 43 percent in 2022, compared to 74 percent in 2016.[1] Too many major changes at once overwhelm employees, and support drops quickly, meaning that the odds of success go down.

Sequencing is the key. Humans can handle only so much change. When too much comes at us all at once, the ability to implement change well suffers. To the receiver, it can be overwhelming. They can feel as if they are trying to drink from a firehose. We end up wasting a lot of "water." What we need to do instead is find one change to make and implement it until it becomes second nature. Then you can continue to do it well as you add the next change.

Another challenge that hinders successful change is lack of clarity. In their book *Switch: How to Change Things When Change Is Hard*, Chip and Dan Heath write that this is the cause of 80 percent of failures.[2]

The Heath brothers tell the story of how Don Berwick, then-CEO and president of the Institute for Healthcare Improvement, set out to tackle the number of deadly medical errors. He announced a prevention initiative, declaring that in 18 months he wanted to save

100,000 lives. (He actually set a date and time: June 14, 2006, at 9:00 a.m.) He proposed six interventions for hospitals to undertake. They were very specific. He made it easy for them to participate. By the deadline, 122,300 lives had been saved. The Heath brothers credit Berwick's clarity and specificity for not just meeting but surpassing the goal. His expression that "some is not a number; soon is not a time" reminds us to get clear on expectations.[2]

We can all strive to be as clear as Don Berwick. Telling people what to do is just the beginning. We must also put some hard timelines in place. Vagueness and uncertainty lead to anxiety and stress and increase the chances that people will make mistakes. People like clear boundaries. They also like leaders who make it easy for them to do their best work.

When leaders aren't being clear, we might mistakenly think people are resisting change. Often they're not being uncooperative; they just didn't hear what we *thought* we said. Clear communication is so important. It promotes teamwork, accountability, and good morale. It reduces workplace drama. It accelerates results and boosts performance.

For these reasons, it's crucial to standardize and implement processes, practices, and leadership throughout the organization. This enables us to create a high-reliability culture with little variance (which is crucial in life-or-death industries like healthcare). It also creates consistent, predictable experiences for employees, which makes it more likely that the workforce will thrive and flourish.

THE DEFIANCE/COMPLIANCE/RELIANCE JOURNEY

People tend to move through change with *defiance, compliance,* and *reliance.* This means that initial defiance of a new idea or a change is normal. People naturally resist change. Our message for leaders is to not be dismayed by this initial defiance. Instead, focus on how to help the person accept or comply with what is being recommended and understand the *why*. Once they've moved through compliance, they will usually land at reliance, meaning that they have come to depend on the new and better way of doing things.

The introduction of peer interviewing of potential new hires provides a good example. When the practice is introduced, there is generally some pushback. Managers express concerns such as "What if they don't hire the right candidate?" They worry about losing that sense of control. But once peer interviewing is underway, they quickly see the benefits. The new hire is likely to be a better fit and be more comfortable because they've already met some of their coworkers. The team feels a big sense of ownership over the new person's success because they had a hand in the hiring process. In fact, once peer interviewing is implemented, leaders would never consider stopping it. They've moved from their initial defiance through compliance and ended up realizing that the change is something they've come to rely on.

Author Wayne Dyer shares that while listening to or reading a message is nice, the *doing* is the key.[3] If we accept this truth without getting lost in the defiance shown by the people we are leading, we can then focus on achieving the desired outcome.

TIPS ON MOVING PEOPLE FROM DEFIANCE THROUGH COMPLIANCE TO RELIANCE

Take time to explain the *why* behind what is being asked. We can't assume that the *why* is obvious. We need to explain it in a way that connects to people's values. For example, Aramark Healthcare shares with environmental service workers how they help prevent falls by making sure certain items are in reach of a patient before they leave the patient's room. This explanation moves a task from "one more thing to do" to "improving patient care." It also reduces call lights, thus saving nurses time (another win). The better the connection to the *why*, the faster the compliance will be.

In healthcare, better patient outcomes are always the *why*. The more the desired behavior is connected to achieving them, the more likely the behavior will be done consistently. Great organizations have "always" behavior, not "usually" or "sometimes" behavior. Once the behavior is connected to clinical outcomes, it connects to a person's values. Then the person cannot *not* do what is needed to help the patient.

Don't try to win over everyone at once. Big kickoff campaigns designed to create a sense of urgency are fine but not the first step. It is better to get a small minority on board at first and stoke their enthusiasm for the change. Plenty of evidence shows that it takes only a small percentage of the population to make a big change happen. Listen to employees for ideas about how best to roll out the process.

Don't sell ideas. Sell successes (and build on them). Try out the change in part of the organization. This helps you adjust your actions based on the experience of those who implement it first. Gather good data on the benefits of the change so that you can quantify the success.

Let people know exactly what to expect. People need to understand what's coming and how it will affect them, and they need to be prepared for it. When people don't know what to expect and don't feel confident that they have what it takes to get through the change, they will quit when things get difficult. When a rollout takes place, help people keep their expectations in check.

Study each employee's personality. Figure out their key drivers. These can vary. As we discussed in chapter 5, every employee is an "N of 1." When we get to know them as unique individuals, we can figure out what motivates them. As we connect with them on this level, compliance is easier to achieve.

Address the "What is in it for me?" factor. This requires the connecting of dots. If people see that a change benefits them personally in some way or aligns with a belief they have, compliance will follow. Benefits can include having more time to do their work better, greater job security, or the satisfaction that comes from better meeting patients' needs.

Assess each person's skills and determine what they need to be successful. Fear of not being successful can create a lack of compliance. A person knows the current way to do something, but they don't know whether they will be successful with the new method or technology. Assuring them that training comes with the required change is vital for moving people to compliance.

Employees may need enhanced technological skills. They may need better communication or time-management skills. Once you've taken the time to identify these skills, you can ensure that employees receive any additional training needed.

Make sure employees are active participants in the change journey. Give them some control over what's happening to them. When people get to make choices during a change, they are a lot more likely to cooperate. People don't like to feel that change is being imposed on them. When they feel that they have a say-so, they'll engage and get on board.

Seek feedback from those being asked to make a change. Ask what barriers may exist. Addressing those barriers will increase the chance of success. Make sure to include all groups that may be affected by the change. For example, a change in nursing protocols can affect every member of the care team.

Be realistic about how long it will take to gain the needed skills. Until the skills are mastered, lots of attention will be paid to each person. More frequent follow-up and accountability can be valuable and may be necessary during a change.

Show empathy for what people are going through. Listen deeply to their fears and concerns about the change. Don't be dismissive or try to talk them out of how they are feeling. They need to feel heard, validated, and supported. Don't try to rush them through this phase. Remember, they are grieving the losses of the "old way," and that will take time. Also, let them know it's normal that things will take longer during the change. Tell them you understand that things may get worse because of the newness of the change before they get better.

Communicate even more than you think you need to. Remember, where there is an information void, people will fill in the blanks themselves. This can lead to a lot of unneeded anxiety and possibly the spread of gossip and misinformation.

Recognize people who are adapting to the new ways. Rewarded and recognized behavior gets repeated. Those who are not adapting will most likely adapt to the change when they see others being recognized for changing.

Meet with those who are not complying and ask what is needed to help them comply. A very small group of people who are not performing as needed can take down a department and an organization.

Apply consequences if needed. About 90 percent of people will respond to the preceding tips. For the remaining 10 percent, consequences for not changing will be necessary. This can be as simple as a question: "I notice you are still not using the new method. Can you help me understand why not?" Noncompliance can eventually lead to a dismissal if the person refuses to adjust to the change.

Don't forget to monitor and measure the change. Otherwise, how will you know whether it's working? Measure both compliance and improvement. Put accountability systems in place to measure compliance. Assuming that the change is intended to lead to better outcomes, measure the improvement. Metrics let people see how far they've come and give you good reasons to celebrate. Connect the dots as to why that improvement is making a difference. This can also help you identify whether the change is bringing any unintended consequences that need to be addressed.

Celebrate successes. (Start with small wins.) At first, set an easy target goal that helps you make progress. This builds people's confidence and enthusiasm and gets momentum going. Once they meet the first goal, make a big deal out of it. They've earned the chance to celebrate! Then while they're still feeling the glow from their success, you can start talking about the next goal. You will find that small wins lead to bigger wins, which in turn lead to even bigger wins.

Instill a "continuous change" mindset. People need to understand that change is not a "one and done" process. It never ends, and that's a good thing, because it's how we grow and thrive.

When people learn, through doing, that a new behavior or process gets results, they see the benefit of compliance. When an organization is great at executing behaviors and processes that lead to better performance, those behaviors and processes will usually become the norm.

Once compliance is in place and the results are achieved, reliance kicks in. This means that people can't fathom going back to the old way because they can now see that the new way works better.

Some people tend to see negative connotations in the words *defiance* and *compliance*. Yet they really aren't negative at all. Both are natural steps in learning and achieving positive change. After all, patients who are the most compliant with their treatment plan have the best outcomes. Those who follow directions get better results.

Guiding people through the compliance, reliance, and defiance process is one of the leader's most important roles. It's not easy, but the rewards can be amazing.

WHEN TO CHANGE COURSE

Change is hard, and we can expect turbulence. Rough spots and resistance aren't reasons to stop and don't mean that the change was the wrong choice. That said, most organizations have stories and examples of changes that ended up being the wrong choice or unexpectedly made things worse. This can happen for several reasons:

- The change caused negative, unintended consequences that were unforeseen.
- Regulatory requirements changed.
- Evidence-based care guidelines changed.

When we have invested a lot of time, energy, and political capital advocating for and initiating a change, it is hard to walk away. People tend to have an escalation of commitment, where they double down on a failed idea because they've already invested so much in it. It takes a lot of humility to stop something that has already started. Sometimes in healthcare, we tend to add more and more processes and activities but don't always stop doing things that aren't serving us anymore.

This is why it is so important to measure the impact of the change. If the negative impact outweighs the positive, it is time to reevaluate whether the initiative should continue.

Successfully implementing change is a lot like running a marathon. It's a huge, rewarding achievement, but it requires that we manage our expectations. You've probably heard that runners tend to "hit the wall" at mile 20. They suddenly feel as if they can't go another step further. If they don't know that this wall exists, they will quit. However, if they know ahead of time that the wall is coming and they have a chance to prepare for it, they'll keep going.

It is the leader's job to prepare people to hit the wall and keep moving through it. When we do, we make it more likely that the plan will be carried through, and we help minimize the anxiety and frustration people feel along the way.

REFERENCES

1. Morain, C. O. and P. Aykens. 2023. "Employees Are Losing Patience with Change Initiatives." *Harvard Business Review*. Published May 9. http://hbr.org/2023/05/employees-are-losing-patience-with-change-initiatives.

2. Heath, C. and D. Heath. 2010. *Switch: How to Change Things When Change Is Hard*. New York: Crown Business.

3. Dyer, W. W. 2009. *There's a Spiritual Solution to Every Problem*. New York: HarperCollins.

Afterword

We are so grateful you have taken time to read *The Human Margin*. Coauthoring a book was new to both of us. We took the opportunity to create a book that is a hybrid: research meets operations. Often when research is presented, people ask for suggestions to improve results. This is much like what happens in clinical care. After the diagnostic results are made available, the next step is a treatment plan. Likewise, when we provide tools and techniques to improve elements such as trust, organizational support, job satisfaction, reward and recognition, and that critical sense of belonging, a frequent question is *What is the research that supports these actions?*

It may sound easy to cover both sides; however, it is not. How can a book include a deep dive into the research and also show how to use that research to achieve high performance? We at times felt as if we were balancing a seesaw. On certain days we would say, "Too much research and not enough solutions." At other times we would say, "Too many tools and not enough research."

Another consideration was "How can the book cover all the different leadership roles in healthcare?" Would a CEO find the book helpful? Would a first-time supervisor find the book useful? We know that all leaders in healthcare have lots in common. While roles and experience vary, the passion and intelligence each leader brings to their role is very similar. This book aims to offer solutions for all those in healthcare.

Add to the equation that one of us comes from the academic view of healthcare while the other comes from operations. Our different perspectives led to many conversations. These conversations required teamwork and trust—exactly the key to creating a great culture. To write about culture and trust, we needed to make sure those things were the foundation for us in coauthoring this book.

We are grateful to the American College of Healthcare Executives for their belief, support, and desire to bring this book to you. We are in awe of each of you. We know that you do not do what you do for money, prestige, or titles. We are in healthcare to make life better for others, even in the toughest of times.

We hope this book is helpful to you on your journey. Be kind to yourself along the way.

Thank you for the privilege to be with you in a small way as you serve with purpose, do worthwhile work, and make a difference.

Katherine and Quint

Acknowledgments

THERE ARE SO many people who paved the way for this book and to whom I owe my sincerest gratitude. I am so grateful to my mentors and teammates at the University of Alabama at Birmingham. Dr. Bob Hernandez let me in the door of the PhD program with such amazing colleagues and mentors. Dr. Nancy Borkowski was my academic "mom" and taught me how to teach, how to write a book, and everything I know about organizational behavior. Dr. Christy Lemak gave me my dream job and freedom and encouragement to explore my passions and try new things. Dr. David Rogers gave tremendous support and mentorship for my research, and he generously invested his funding from the ProAssurance Corporation to provide resources for our team in the UAB Medicine Office of Wellness. My students and postdocs, Dr. Alejandra Colón-López and Dr. Laurence Boitet, were amazing partners in every aspect of our work. Chuck Stokes believed in me and encouraged me to step out of my academic comfort zone to get more engaged with the industry. I also owe a very special thank-you to Dr. Dan Gentry, president and CEO of the Association for University Programs in Health Administration (AUPHA), for introducing me to Quint. I am so grateful to Quint for his collaboration, generosity, and support through this process. On a personal note, I have tremendous gratitude for my late mother, a nurse and educator, whose mentorship, guidance, humor, pursuit of excellence, and passion for teaching have influenced almost every page of this book. Lastly, a huge thank-you to my husband and children for their unending love, support, and patience.

Katherine Meese

THANK YOU TO Dr. Katherine Meese for bringing great research and thought leadership to the field. Her passion to keep people first and foremost in care delivery is vital to the future of patient care. Thanks also to Dottie DeHart, who has worked with me for 20 years on books, columns, and articles. She was vital in combining the research with the operational solutions. Special thanks to my colleague Dan Collard. I am so fortunate to learn from him. And to the people who have allowed me to be on the journey of skill development these many decades, I am grateful for your trust, patience, and teachings.

Thank you to the leaders who have bought this book for current and potential leaders in their organizations. If you received this book from a leader in your organization, you have a good one. To those who purchased the book in the search to feel better about the role they are in: Years ago in my first supervisory role, I bought the book *In Search of Excellence: Lessons from America's Best-Run Companies* by Thomas J. Peters and Robert H. Waterman Jr. It helped me not to feel alone and provided some ways to be a better leader.

I join Katherine in thanking Dr. Dan Gentry of AUPHA. Dan, along with Dr. Anthony Stanowski, president and CEO of the Commission on Accreditation of Healthcare Management Education (CAHME), has graciously allowed me to still be in the educational field in healthcare administration.

I also wish to thank the following:

The American College of Healthcare Executives (ACHE) for being the backbone of healthcare leadership.

All the fire starters for keeping the flame burning even in the most difficult times.

The hundreds of organizations who continue to be all-in on making healthcare a healing place for patients, staff, and physicians.

Quint Studer

Appendix

THIS BOOK COMBINES findings from the academic literature in many industries, as well as original research, with over 10,000 observations that chronicle the healthcare employee experience over the course of several years. You can read more about the research design and approach in the peer-reviewed articles listed below.

Meese, K. A., L. M. Boitet, J. J. Schmidt, N. Borkowski, and K. L. Sweeney. 2023. "Exploring National Trends and Organizational Predictors of Violence and Mistreatment from Patients and Visitors." *Journal of Healthcare Management.*

Boitet, L. M., K. A. Meese, M. Hays, C. A. Gorman, K. L. Sweeney, and D. A. Rogers. 2023. "Burnout, Moral Distress, and Compassion Fatigue as Correlates of Post-Traumatic Stress Symptoms in Clinical and Non-Clinical Healthcare Workers." *Journal of Healthcare Management.*

Meese, K. A., L. M. Boitet, K. L. Sweeney, L. Nassetta, M. Mugavero, B. Hidalgo, R. Reamey, and D. A. Rogers. 2023. "Still Exhausted: The Role of Residual Caregiving Fatigue on Women in Medicine and Science Across the Pipeline." *Journal of Medical Internet Research.* https://www.jmir.org/2023/1/e47629.

Boitet, L. M., K. A. Meese, A. Colón-López, K. L. Sweeney, and D. A. Rogers. 2023. "Perceptions of Safety Versus Actual Exposure Across the Entire Healthcare Team During COVID-19." *Journal of Healthcare Risk Management*. doi: 10.1002/jhrm.21542

Boitet L. M., K. A. Meese, A. Colón-López, K. L. Sweeney, L. M. Schwiebert, and D. A. Rogers. 2023. "An Investigation of Organizational Correlates of Distress in Non-Clinician Biomedical Researchers in the United States." *Journal of Multidisciplinary Healthcare* 2023(16): 333–43. https://doi.org/10.2147/JMDH.S399517.

Meese, K. A., A. Colón-López, A. P. Montgomery, L. M. Boitet, D. A. Rogers, and P. A. Patrician. 2022. "Rules of Engagement: The Role of Mistreatment from Patients in the Nurse, Physician and Advanced Practice Provider Experience." *Patient Experience Journal* 9(2): 36–45.

Meese, K. A., C. Dobbins, A. Colón-López, F. Van Pelt, D. A. Rogers, and K. Flood. 2022. "Accountable Care Team Membership and Distress: Is Accountable Care Team Membership Associated with Lower Distress During a Crisis?" *Journal of Hospital Management and Health Policy*. https://jhmhp.amegroups.com/article/view/7331.

Colón-López, A., K. A. Meese, A. P. Montgomery, P. A. Patrician, D. A. Rogers, and G. A. Burkholder. 2022. "Unique Stressors in a Global Pandemic: A Mixed Methods Study About Unique Causes of Distress Among Healthcare Team Members During COVID-19." *Journal of Hospital Management and Health Policy*. doi: 10.21037/jhmhp-21-69.

Meese, K. A., A. G. Hall, S. S. Feldman, A. Colón-López, D. A. Rogers, and J. A. Singh. 2022. "Physician, Nurse, and Advanced Practice Provider Perspectives on the Rapid Transition to Inpatient and Outpatient Telemedicine." *Telemedicine Reports* 3(1): 7–14.

Meese, K. A., A. Colón-López, R. Dill, G. A. Naik, P. J. Cendoma, and D. A. Rogers. 2021. "Perceptions of Inequitable Compensation

Reductions Among Healthcare Workers During Covid-19." *Journal of Health Care Finance* 48(2): 1–15.

Meese, K. A., A. Colón-López, J. A. Singh, G. A. Burkholder, and D. A. Rogers. 2021. "Healthcare Is a Team Sport: Stress, Resilience, and Correlates of Well-Being Among Health System Employees in a Crisis." *Journal of Healthcare Management* 66(4): 304–22.

Index

Note: Italicized page locators refer to exhibits.

Briefing huddle: in Circle Up model, 150–51
"Bright Ideas" programs, 72–73
Brown, Brené, 139
Bullying, 142
Burnout, 4, 137; contagious nature of, 120; distress and, 16; drivers of, 132–33; lack of autonomy and, 107; lack of boundaries and, 112; lack of clarity about roles and, 139; lack of fairness and, 97; low, Net Promoter Score and, 29; preventing, 26; stress and trauma compared with, 121–23; three dimensions of, 121; turnover and, 24, 25

Calling: to be in healthcare work, 4, 108
Camaraderie: encouraging, 147
Career development: prioritizing, for Generation Z employees, 156. See also Leadership development
Caregivers: addressing psychological well-being of, 26; burnout and distress among, 16; ensuring fairness for, 100–102; exodus of, 14–15; fostering sense of belonging for, 47; inefficiencies and, 112–14; peer support for, 148–49; recognition for, 74–75; use of term in text, 9. See also Nurses; Physicians
Celebrations: coworker bonds and, 57; powerful effect of, 70–71
Ceremonies, 70–71
Challenge demands: increasing, 114
Change: categories of response to, 168; listening to employees about, 173; loss linked to, 168; as the norm in healthcare, 167
Change management, 10, 167–77; challenges with, 167–69; defiance/compliance/reliance journey and, 171–76; lack of clarity as derailer of, 170–71; predictable path in, 169; sequencing and, 170; trust and, 167; when to change course, 176–77
CHORES 1st for building trust, 35–37; competency and consistency in, 35; expectations in, 36; 1st in, 36–37; honesty in, 35; own your mistakes in, 36; relationship in, 36; safety in, 36
Circle Up model: critical success factors for, 151–52; peer support and, 150–52; results tied to, 152
Civility, 140
Clarity: change hindered by lack of, 170–71; good communication and, 78, 81; role-related, lack of, 139
Cleveland Clinic: bright ideas welcomed at, 73; complimenting employees at, 75
Clinical outcomes: well-being and, 120

Clinicians: use of term in text, 9. See also Caregivers; Nurses; Physicians
Coaching: good communication and, 91; recognition and, 63; sense of belonging and, 54
Collaboration, 144; across silos, 140; encouraging, 147; inter-departmental, 147; in leadership development, 165
Collegiality: great coworkers and, 143
Communication, 10, 55, 77–95; asking people how they want to get information, 81; being heard, creating best odds for, 84–87; cascading information for smart sequencing, 85–86; change management and, 175; clear, change and, 171; consistent messaging and, 85; difficulties with, factors related to, 79–80; fostering sense of belonging through, 53; getting intentional with messaging and actions, 83–84; good thriving organizations and, 78–79; importance of, 77; methods of, 81–83; open, trust and, 33; playing offense on, 80–83; positive, making time for, 91–93; questions and, 87–88; red flags in, watching for, 80; responsibility narrated in process of, 83; simple and clear messaging, 84–85; storytelling and, 94–95; teach-back method in, 85; timing of messages in, 86; trust-building questions, 88–89; as a two-way street, 87–88; untold stories, 86–87; with your upper brain, 93–94
Community: building, 57; burnout and lack of, 133
Compassion fatigue, 148
Compensation, 22, 24
Competence: in CHORES 1st for building trust, 35
Competencies: belonging and, 48
Compliance: change management and, 171–72, 176
Compliments, 66
Concern, expressing, 149
Confidentiality issues: mental health assistance and, 129
Connell, Eric, 90
Consistency: in CHORES 1st for building trust, 35
"Continuous change" mindset, instilling, 176
Control: burnout and lack of, 132
Conversations: about well-being, 123; creating safe environments for, 124; healing power of, 127
Covey, Stephen M. R.: on trust, 33

COVID-19 pandemic, 132; caregiver exodus and, 4, 14–15; distress scores and, 26–27, *27*; mortality salience and, 14

Coworker relationships, 10; fostering, importance of, 56–58; great, qualities of, 142–44; great, tools and tactics for, 145–48; sense of belonging and, 52; supporting healthy, 141–42

Critical care nurses: COVID-19 pandemic and exodus of, 14–15

Critical thinking, 162

Cross-functional projects, 147

Culture: of accountability, coworker relationships and, 56; of honesty, trust, and psychological safety, 146; making peer support a part of, 150–52; of recognition, payoff with, 62–63; of recognition, rich and sustainable, 67–70; strong coworker relationships and, 142; toxic, turnover and, 22, *23*; of wellness, great leadership and, 134

Cynicism, 121

Debriefing huddle: in Circle Up model, 151

Decision-making: fairness and, 101; sense of belonging and, 55–56; trust and, 37

Defiance/compliance/reliance journey: to change, 171–72; moving through, tips on, 172–76

Demands, reducing, 111–14; clear guidelines for staff, 112–14; organizing use of technology, 112; reducing duplicative documentation, 111; setting boundaries, 112

Departmental collaboration, 147

Department of Veterans Affairs: annual employee survey, 25

Depression: caregivers and, 16; lack of clarity about roles and, 139

Development plans: sense of belonging and, 54

DiSC, 145

Discrimination, 103, 119

Dissatisfaction: lack of clarity about roles and, 139

Distress: burnout and, 16; caregivers and, 26; extending help to employees in, 123–26; looking for signs of, in colleagues, 123, 149; reducing sources of, 120; top 10 predictors of, 26–28, *27*

Distrust, 35, 79

Diversity: promoting, 147; reducing, unconscious biases and, 102

Diversity, equity, and inclusion: women leaders and commitment to, 17

Documentation burdens: reducing, 111

Drug shortages, 110

Duplicative documentation: reducing, 111

Dyer, Wayne, 172

EAP services, 133

Edmondson, Amy, 140

Educational programs, 6. *See also* Leadership development; Training

Efficiency gains: spending wisely, 134

EHRs. *See* Electronic health records (EHRs)

Elective surgeries: pandemic and cancellations of, 15

Electronic health records (EHRs): workload burdens and, 112

e-mails, 82

Emotional bank accounts: building for employees, 61, 75; good communication and, 78

Emotional exhaustion, 25, 120, 121. *See also* Burnout

Emotionally intelligent leadership: good communication and, 79

Empathy, 34; change management and, 174; good communication and, 78

Employee resource groups, 147

Employees: as active participants in change process, 174; experienced, losses related to replacement of, 22; Generation Z, career development for, 156; replacement costs and, 22; use of term in text, 9. *See also* Staff and staffing

Empowering leaders: aim of, 114–15; traits of, *115*

Engagement, 137, 144; belonging and, 50; empowering leadership and, 115; fairness and, 100; good communication and, 77, 78; good coworker relationships and, 142; honesty of senior leaders and, 25; increasing resources and, 109–10; in PERMA model, 3; questions and, 87; well-being and, 120

Equality: pursuing equity over, 98

Equity Theory (Adams), 99

Evidence-based approach: to maximizing the human margin, 8–10

Examples, setting for great coworker relationships, 146

Expectations: change rollouts and, 173; in CHORES 1st for building trust, 36; clarifying, 140

Expendability: countering feeling of, 4

Experienced employees: replacing, losses related to, 22

Extrinsic motivators: belonging and, 50

Fairness, 10, 56, 97–104; building trust with, 97; burnout and lack of, 97; creating environment of, two principles of, 98–99; great coworker relationships and, 146–47; inputs and outputs relative to, 99–102; managing perceptions of, 101–2; perceived lack of, burnout and, 133; in the process and in the results, 98–99; unconscious bias and, 102–4

Favoritism: being mindful about, 101

Favors: connecting through requesting, 55–56

Feedback: change management and, 174; good communication and, 91; good coworker relationships and, 142; honest, 35; improving efficiency and, 134; openness to, great coworkers and, 143; sense of belonging and, 54; unconscious biases and, 104

Female physicians: suicide and, 16

Financial margin, 1

Flexibility: worker expectations and, 17; in work schedules, autonomy and, 108

Flourishing: PERMA model of, 3

Follow up and follow through, peer support and, 149

Forgiveness: benefits of, 42; trust and, 42

Friends in workplace, importance of, 56, 141–42

Frisina, Michael E., 93

Frisina, Robert, 93

Frontline service workers: recognition for, 74

Fun: great coworker relationships and sense of, 147

Gehrig, Lou, 67

Generation Z employees: prioritizing career development for, 156

Getting Rid of Stupid Stuff (GROSS), 133

Goals: great coworker relationships and emphasis on, 146

Golden question: asking, 90–91

Goodwill: building with good communication, 91–93

Gossip, 86, 119, 142; avoiding, 57; countering with good communication, 79; nixing, to support great coworker relationships, 146; positive vs. negative, 42

Gratitude, 62, 150

Great Resignation, 14

Grief: change and, 168

GROSS. See Getting Rid of Stupid Stuff (GROSS)

Group norms: establishing, 56–57

Group recognition: using care with, 70

Guidelines: unclear, 112–14

Handoffs, 112, 139

Hazard pay, 15

Health: chronic stress and impact on, 121; loneliness and impact on, 47–48; recognition and benefits for, 62; status on social ladder correlated with, 98. See also Mental health; Wellness/well-being

Healthcare: change as the norm in, 167; defined, 1; as a team sport, 9, 137, 152

Healthcare industry: constantly evolving nature of, 157; external environment and impact on, 17–18; size of, 2; special nature of, 1

Healthcare workforce: community, healthy work, and, 3

Healthy teams, 10

Healthy work: creating, 120, 132–34

Heath, Chip, 170

Heath, Dan, 170

Helpfulness: great coworkers and, 143

Henley, William Ernest, 107

High-performance organizations: creating healthy work in, 134

High-reliability culture: clear communication and, 171

Hiring: fostering a sense of belonging and, 47. See also Recruitment

Honesty, 34; in CHORES 1st for building trust, 35; creating culture of, 146; great coworkers and, 143; of senior leaders, employee engagement and, 25. See also Trust

Horn, Marcia, 54

Housing prices: inflation of, 15

Houston Methodist: belonging supported at, 55–56

Huddles: briefing, in Circle Up model, 150–51; daily, 82–83; debriefing, in Circle Up model, 151; recognition and, 67

Human margin, 1–10; aging of the population and, 16–17; burnout and distress and, 16; caregiver exodus, 14–15; defined, 2; improving, elements in, 10; inflation and unemployment dynamic, 15; maximizing, evidence-based approach to, 8–10; midlevel leaders and, 6; strengthening with leadership development, 165; strength of, questions to ask about, 2; tipping point with, 7–8; what we aim for and, 2–5; wisely spending efficiency gains and, 134

Humility, 34; changing course and need for, 177; great coworkers and, 143

Humor, 150

Hyperarousal: as side effect of trauma, 122

Improvements: seeking suggestions for, 134

Inclusion: promoting and supporting, 47, 147

Inclusive teams, 103
Individualized consideration: transformational leadership and, 100
Inefficiencies: identifying and eliminating, 112–14, 133
Inequity, 133; lack of fairness and seriousness of, 97; perceived, correlation with status and, 98; retention and addressing sources of, 98; unconscious biases and, 103, 104
Inflation: unemployment and, 15
Information void: change management and, 175
In-groups: being watchful for formation of, 54; out-groups and, 49–50
Innovation: recognition and, 72–73
Inputs: determination of fairness and, 102; perceptions of inequity and, 99, 100
Institute for Healthcare Improvement, 89, 170
Institutional knowledge: experienced employee replacement and loss of, 22
Integrity, 34, 37
International Cancer Advocacy Network, 54
Intrinsic motivators: belonging and, 50

Job crafting, 109–14, 116; description of, 109; empowering employees for, 116; increasing resources and, 109–11; reducing demands and, 111–14
Job Demands-Resources theory, 109, 133
Job dissatisfaction: lack of clarity about roles and, 139
Job insecurity, 119
Job rotation, 147
Job satisfaction: forgiveness of leaders and, 44; Precision Leader Development™ and, 163; well-being and, 28
Judgment: listening without, 150

Kaplan, Jay, 126, 127
Kindness: for ourselves, 131
Kotter, John, 169
Krauss, Sister Irene, 1

Labor costs: inflation and, 15
Laughter, 150
Leaders: accessible, sense of belonging and, 54; good communication and, 77; great, investing in, 163; recognizing, 74–75; tough questions and, 40–42, 80; training, 7; vulnerability in, sharing, 129–30. See also Midlevel leaders; Senior leaders
Leadership: empowering, 114–15, 115; foundational skills, examples of, 160;

foundational skills rating, sample survey, 161; great, culture of wellness and, 134; heavy burden of, 43; transactional, 156; transformational, 156; trauma-informed, 122–23; turnover intention and quality of, 24–25
Leadership assessment, four components of, 159, 159–62; leadership skills assessment, 159, 159–60; learning style, 159, 162; personality and behavior assessment, 159, 162; problem-solving ability, 159, 162
Leadership development, 10, 155–65; collaborative factor in, 165; complex workplace and need for, 156; effective, as anxiety reducer, 156; importance of, 155; new way to think about, 157; organizational performance and, 156–57; OSAR™ approach, 163, 164, 165; Precision Leader Development™, 157–62; strengthening the human margin with, 165. See also Training
Leadership meetings: as communication avenue, 81
Leading With Your Upper Brain (Frisina), 93
Learning styles: awareness of, 159, 168
Listening: asking good questions and, 87; without judgment, 150
Loneliness: profound ill health effects of, 47–48
Loop, Dr. Floyd (Fred), 73, 75
Loss: change linked to, 168
"Lower brain": limitations of, 93

Managers: complex workplace and, 156; inexperience of, 155–56
Marginalized groups: negative effects of unconscious biases and, 103
Maslach, Christina, 121
Maslow's hierarchy of needs: autonomy and self-actualization in, 107
Mastery: humans motivated by, 107, 108
Meaning and purpose: healthcare work and, 14; in PERMA model, 3, 4
Medical errors: deadly, Berwick's goal in saving 100,000 lives from, 170–71
Meetings: getting intentional with messaging and actions after, 83–84
memento mori: meaning of, 13
Mental health: assistance, 127, 128; recognizing issues in employees, 119; reducing stigma of, 128–29; supporting in employees, 26
Mentoring: unconscious biases and, 103. See also Coaching
Metrics: change management and, 175, 177
Micro-empathy: in Circle Up model, 151

Role conflict: reducing, 139–40
Role-playing: for "caring conversations," 123
Rounding: recognition and, 66; Relationship Rounding, 91; as a trust builder, 37; weekly, 82

Safety: in CHORES 1st for building trust, 36. *See also* Psychological safety
Salaries, 15, 24
Scope-of-practice laws, 139
Scribes, 112
Self-actualization: autonomy and, 107
Self-awareness, 159, 160
Self-compassion, 131
Self-confidence: Precision Leader Development™ and, 163
Seligman, M.: PERMA model of, 3
Senior leaders: crucial role of, in employee engagement, 25; trust cap, closing, 38–39; trust gap, cause of, 38; trust in, importance of, 34
Senior leadership: trust in, 7
Sequencing: organizational change and, 170
Shadowing, 147
Shortages in labor force: COVID-19 pandemic and, 15
SHRM. *See* Society for Human Resource Management (SHRM)
Silence: avoiding with shared stories, 150
"Sizzle to fizzle" phenomenon: change initiatives and, 169
Skills: mastering, change management and, 174
Social connections: through peer support, 148–49; workplace, importance of, 141
Social hierarchy: perceived inequity and negative changes in, 98
Social resources, 109, 110
Society for Human Resource Management (SHRM): Workplace Romance and Relationships Survey, 56
Sonic boom, 169
Staff and staffing: inflation, unemployment dynamics, and, 15; shortages, challenges related to, 21
Standards of behavior: recognition connected to, 68; setting, for supportive work environment, 152
Standards of Behavior document, 56–57; tips for, 144–45
Stigma of mental health: reducing, 128–29
Stoic philosophers, 13
Stories: untold, 86–87
Storytelling: harnessing power of, 94–95; promoting legacy of organization through, 95

StrengthsFinder, 145
Stress: brain functioning and, 26, 120, 121; burnout and trauma compared with, 121–23; chronic, 128; defining, 121; helping employees develop understanding of, 124; role conflicts and, 140; supervisory positions and, 7
Structural resources, 109, 110
Successes: celebrating, change management and, 175; selling, and building on, 173
Suicide: caregivers and, 16
Supervisors: trust in, 34
Supervisory positions: stress and, 7
Supply chain disruptions, challenges related to, 110
Supply costs: inflation and, 15
Switch: How to Change Things When Change Is Hard (Heath & Heath), 170

Talent: attracting, trust and, 33
Teach-back method: key points and, 85
Teams: appreciating contributions of, 66; diverse and inclusive, 103; fostering great coworker relationships on, tools and tactics for, 145–48; fostering psychological safety for, 140–41; great coworkers on, qualities of, 142–45; healthy, working on, 137–38; homogeneous, underperformance of, 49; job crafting and, 116; midlevel leadership, winning organizations and, 5, 7; peer support and, 148–52; reducing role conflict on, 139–40; setting conditions for success of, 138–40; Standards of Behavior for, 144–45; supporting healthy coworker relationships on, 141–42; tackling role ambiguity in, 138–39
Thank-you notes, 69–70
Threats: brain and response to, 119
Tough questions and leaders: answering, 40–41, 80; getting clarity around, 42; unexpected questions, 41–42
Town hall meetings: as communication avenue, 81–82
Toxic behavior: reduced, strong coworker relationships and, 142
Toxic corporate culture: employee exodus and, 22, 23
Toxic positivity: optimism *vs.*, 93; watching out for, 92–93
Training, 133; change management and, 174; leaders, 7; narrowing focus of, 165; new way of, 157; sense of belonging and, 54; to shore up "good coworker" skills, 146; unconscious biases and, 103. *See also* Leadership development

About the Authors

With over a decade of experience in health-care and research, **Katherine A. Meese, PhD,** is a leader in the field of organizational behavior, well-being, and delivery models that enhance organizational learning. She is an assistant professor in the department of health services administration at the University of Alabama at Birmingham (UAB) and is the director of research at the UAB Medicine Office of Wellness, where she oversees the evaluation of evidence-based interventions to improve the health and performance of healthcare workers.

She also teaches and mentors students in UAB's many nationally recognized programs. She has coauthored two textbooks on organizational behavior in healthcare, as well as multiple book chapters and peer-reviewed articles. Her mission is to put the human back into healthcare and to inspire the next generation of healthcare leaders.

Quint Studer, MSE, is a lifelong student of leadership. He has a gift for translating complex strategies into doable behaviors that allow organizations to achieve long-term success.

Quint is the author of 15 books. His first title, *BusinessWeek* bestseller *Hardwiring Excellence*, is one of the most-read leadership books ever written for healthcare. Two of his other books—*Results That Last* and *The Busy Leader's Handbook*—became *Wall Street Journal* bestsellers. He also recently released *The Calling: Why Healthcare Is So Special*, which is aimed at helping healthcare professionals keep their sense of passion and purpose high, and *Sundays with Quint*, which is a collection of his most popular leadership columns. His newest book, *Rewiring Excellence: Hardwired to Rewired*, looks at which widely embraced behaviors and processes may need "rewiring" in response to our rapidly shifting environment and offers guidance on making them doable.

In his most recent venture to serve healthcare, he founded Healthcare Plus Solutions Group (HPSG) along with longtime colleague Dan Collard. The mission of the organization is to have a positive impact on those who receive care and those who provide care. HPSG specializes in helping healthcare organizations diagnose and treat their most urgent pain points in order to achieve and sustain results. For more information, please visit www.healthcareplussg.com.